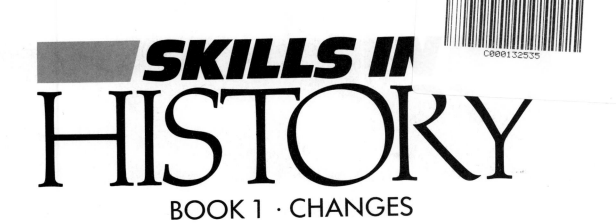

SKILLS IN HISTORY

BOOK 1 · CHANGES

C000132535

Series Editor: PAUL SHUTER

PAUL SHUTER   JOHN CHILD

 HEINEMANN EDUCATIONAL BOOKS

Heinemann Educational Books Ltd
22 Bedford Square, London WC1B 3HH

LONDON   EDINBURGH   MELBOURNE   AUCKLAND
SINGAPORE   KUALA LUMPUR   NEW DELHI
IBADAN   NAIROBI   JOHANNESBURG
PORTSMOUTH (NH)   KINGSTON

© Paul Shuter and John Child 1987

First published 1987
Reprinted 1987 (twice)
Reprinted 1988 (with amendments)

British Library Cataloguing in Publication Data

Shuter, Paul
   Skills in History.
   1. History
   I. Title II. Child, John
   900   D21.
   ISBN 0-435-31862-4

Designed and typeset by
The Pen and Ink Book Company Ltd, London

Printed in Great Britain by Butler & Tanner Ltd, Frome,
and London

ISBN 0 435 31865 9
(Teacher's Set)

We have noticed that authors often dedicate
their books to their wives; now we know why.

For Jane and Marian

Other titles in the *Skills in History* series:

Book 2 Revolutions

This book looks at two different types of revolution; one
political, the other economic. Part One covers England in
the seventeenth century. Part Two describes Britain's
Industrial Revolution.

Book 3 The Twentieth Century

Book 3 will be extremely valuable for third-year work and
for GCSE. It offers concept-focused double-page spreads
on main areas of modern world history and a final section
on some of the advantages and the problems of using
twentieth-century sources.

Contents

Acknowledgements

The authors and publishers would like to thank the following for permission to reproduce photographs on the pages indicated:

The Archaeological Journal, Royal Archaeological Institute: p. 87.
Ashmolean Museum, Oxford: p. 60.
Barnado Film Library: p. 19.
BBC Hulton Picture Library: pp. 103 and 117 (*left*).
John Bethell: p. 17 (*lower right*).
Malcolm Booker and Heinemann Educational Books: p. 5 (*top left*).
The British Library: pp. 15 (*middle*), 62, 96 (*lower middle*), 110 and 111.
The Trustees of the British Museum: pp. 4, 5 (*top right and lower*), 15 (*top and lower*), 21, 26, 27 (*left*), 34 (*left*), 40, 41, 52, 61, 104, 106 and 114 (*lower*).
James Campbell and the Phaidon Press: p. 50 (*left*).
The Governing Body of Christ Church College, Oxford: p. 17 (*lower left*).
Peter Clayton: pp. 31, 32 (*right*) and 74.
The College of Arms: p. 101 (*lower*).
Mr Simon Wingfield Digby, Sherborne Castle: p. 112 (*lower*).
C. M. Dixon: pp. 32 (*left*) and 34 (*right*).
The Governors of Dulwich College: p. 115.
English Heritage: pp. 44 (*top and lower*) and 47.
Mary Evans Picture Library: pp. 101 (*middle*).
Grafton Books: p. 12 (*lower*).
Grosvenor Museum, Chester: p. 27 (*right*).
Eric Hall: p. 96 (*lower*).
Historic Buildings and Monuments Commission for England: pp. 91 and 107.
C. Walter Hodges: p. 118 (*right*).
Michael Holford: p. 96 (*upper middle*).
W. T. Jones: p. 51.
Nigel and Mary Kerr: p. 94 (*left and top*).
Kunsthistorisches Museum, Vienna: p. 12 (*middle*).
The Master and Fellows, Magdalene College, Cambridge: p. 22.
Manchester City Art Galleries: p. 12 (*top*).
The Mansell Collection: pp. 24, 28, 29, 55, 101 (*top*), 108 (*top*), 112 (*top*), 114 (*top*), 116, 117 (*lower*) and 122.
The *Mary Rose* Trust: pp. 22 and 23.
Ministry of Defence: p. 71 (*top*) [Crown Copyright Reserved].
Museum of Antiquities of the University and Society of Antiqueries of Newcastle-upon-Tyne: pp. 44 (*middle*) and 45 (*lower*).
National Parks and Monuments Branch, Dublin: p. 65.
National Portrait Gallery, London: p. 108 (*lower*).
The Northbourne Collection, Ashmolean Museum, Oxford: p. 50.
Joan Nunn and the Herbert Press: p. 13 (*top*).
Ivy Pinchbeck and Margaret Hewitt/Routledge & Kegan Paul: p. 13 (*middle*).
Procter & Gamble Ltd: p. 9.
The Roundwood Press at Kineton, Warwick: pp. 17 (*top left, middle left, and middle right*).
The Board of Trustees of the Royal Armouries: p. 100.
Royal Commission on the Historical Monuments of England: pp. 71 (*lower*) and 90.
David Sylvester: p. 13 (*lower*).
The Marquess of Tavistock, and the Trustees of the Bedford Estates: p. 113.
University of Cambridge Committee for Aerial Photography: pp. 16, 71 (*middle*) and 96 (*top*).
University Library, Utrecht: p. 114 (*top*).
University Museum of National Antiquities, Oslo: pp. 53 and 66.
Ville de Bayeux: pp. 76, 79, 80, 86 and 87.
Weidenfeld & Nicolson Archives: p. 95.
Werner Forman Archive: p. 34.
R. J. A. Wilson: p. 42.

What is Chronology?

Activity

What is wrong with the cartoon story you have just read?
Work out what you think happened.

Historians always have a story to tell, and stories do not make sense unless what happened is told in the right order. So one of the first things a historian does, whatever their interest, is work out the **order in which things happened**. You will not have been able to answer the questions about the cartoon without working out the right order for the pictures.

Sometimes knowing the order that things happened in is so important that it can change the story:

The body in the room

There is a body of a murdered man on the floor in a room.
A man screamed.
A man went into a room.
A man left a room.

Activity

Make up two paragraphs using the events in the box above. Use only the events given, but change the order in which things happen so that you produce two different stories.

It is not just historians who need to know exactly when something happened. We often need to know when something is going to happen, or has happened, in our everyday lives. This was true in the past as well, and is the reason why one of the first things early civilisations, like Babylon and Egypt, did was to work out a way of measuring time. We call these systems **calendars**. The calendar we use in Britain divides time up into days, weeks, months and years. To make the calendar easier to use, the days are given names and numbers, the months names and the years numbers. Historians use this system as well. For instance, we say the Gunpowder Plot was a plan to blow up Parliament on 5 November 1605, which is also what the people living at the time would have called that day.

The study of time and dates is called **chronology**. To put something in chronological order is to organise it so that the earliest things come first, and so on, until the latest things come last. Chronology is important to historians, but history is more than just chronology. A list of things in the order that they happened would not be very interesting. Historians need to understand chronology as a first step so that they can work out why things happened.

One good way of showing the order in which things happen is a **time-line**. This can be used to show the events of a day, or whole centuries, depending on the scale of the line.

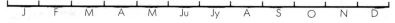

This line could be used to mark the events of your school day. Something that happens at 9.30 a.m. goes in the middle of the space between 9 and 10. On this line the scale is one hour for each space.

By changing the scale, a line could be drawn showing the events of a whole year:

Questions

1 What is chronological order?

2 Why do historians need to know the order in which events happened?

3 Why is a time-line useful?

4 Draw a time-line to show:

   a the things that happened to you last week;
   b the most important events in your life.

Dividing History into Bits

A Bronze Age cauldron.

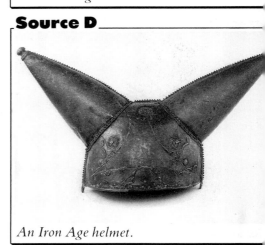

An Iron Age helmet.

There have been people living on the Earth for about the last 600,000 years. This is a very long time indeed. Historians need some way of dividing up this length of time so that they know what 'bit' they are talking about. If someone asked you where you live, you would not say, 'The Earth', and leave it at that. You could give the continent in which you live, and the country, the county, the city, town or village, and even the street and house number. Historians have divided up time in the same way that geographers have divided up the world.

Historians divide time up in various different ways. They talk about the **prehistoric period**. This means the period before writing was discovered. It is called prehistoric because at one time historians thought they could write only about civilisations that had left written records which could be studied. In the same way that Europe is a continent which is split up into lots of different countries, the prehistoric period is a 'time-continent', and it can be split up, too. You have probably heard of the **Stone Age**, the **Bronze Age** and the **Iron Age**. These are all divisions of the prehistoric period. Because there are no written records, historians study the things that have survived, especially tools, and the best way of dividing up the prehistoric period is by what people made their tools from.

Stone Age	Bronze Age	Iron Age

←—————————————Prehistoric Period—————————————→

However, this diagram is not quite right. Historical periods were not all the same length. The Stone Age lasted an especially long time. More than 99 per cent of human history in the prehistoric period was spent in the Stone Age. If we show the same information on a time-line – see below – it is very different.

There is another complication about these divisions. They describe the way that people lived, but different people in different places developed at different rates. This means that while people in Britain were still in the Stone Age, people in other areas such as the Middle East had moved into the Bronze Age.

So far we have looked only at the prehistoric period. Historians use lots of other ways of dividing up time. One way is to choose what seems to be the most important happening of the period. The **Reformation**, for instance, is the name given to the period when the reform of the Church happened in most European countries. Perhaps in the future

The prehistoric period showing the Stone, Bronze and Iron Ages.

Questions

1 List the objects in Sources A – F in chronological order. Explain why you have put them in the order that you have.

2 Draw a time-line of your own life, like the personal time-line opposite. See if you can divide your life up into sections. The words historians use for these sections are 'period', 'age' and 'era'.

A time-line of the prehistoric period showing the Stone, Bronze and Iron Ages.

←————————————————————————— Stone Age (600 000 yea

Source B

...istory textbook published in 1980.

Source C

A flint hand axe.

Source E

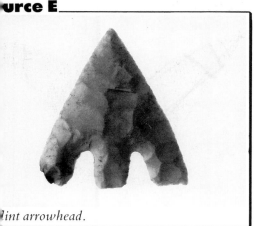

...lint arrowhead.

Source F

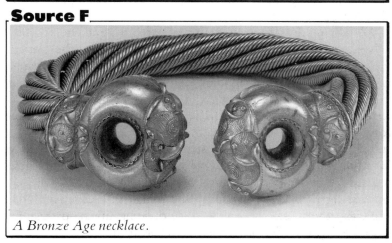

A Bronze Age necklace.

A personal time-line.

Nappy Period

| – 1 | 2 | 3 | 4 | 5 | 6 | 7 | 8 | 9 | 10 | 11 | 12 |

our time will be called the Space Age or the Computer Age.

Another way of dividing up time is by who was ruling the country. The names of families of kings and queens are often used. In England and Wales we talk of the Tudor Age or the Stuart Age. Historians in other countries do not divide up their country's history by who ruled Britain. They divide time up by the families of their own rulers.

English history, 1066–1980, divided into royal families.

Lancaster York

| Normans | Plantagenets | | Tudors | Stuarts | Hanover | Windsor |

| 1000 | 1066 | 1100 | 1154 | 1200 | 1300 | 1399 | 1400 | 1461 1485 | 1500 | 1603 | 1600 | 1714 | 1700 | 1800 | 1917 | 1900 | 2000 |

Chinese history 500 BC – AD 1911, divided into the families of the emperors (called dynasties).

| Chou (warring states period) | Ch'in | Early Han | Later Han | Six Dynasties | Sui | T'ang | Five Dynasties | North Sung | South Sung | Yuan | Ming | Ch'ing (Manchus) | Kuomintang | CCP |

| 500 | 300 | 100 BC | AD 100 | 300 | 500 | 700 | 900 | 1100 | 1300 | 1500 | 1700 | 1900 |

Bronze and Iron Age (3 000 years)

Counting Years

Historians often need to be much more accurate than just giving the name of a period during which something happened. They use the number of the year. For instance, Columbus discovered America in 1492. But 1,492 years from when? When did people start to count from?

Christian countries all use a system of counting years which starts from the birth of Christ. They have used this method since AD 525 when Dionysius Exiguus, a monk, worked out how many years had passed since Christ's birth. We should say that Columbus discovered America in AD 1492. AD stands for Anno Domini, which is Latin for 'In the year of our Lord'. So Columbus arrived in America 1,492 years after the birth of Christ. History, of course, does not begin with the birth of Christ, so we also count years backwards from that point. Something which happened ten years before the birth of Christ is said to have happened in 10 BC ('before Christ'). Ten years before 10 BC was 20 BC. The bigger the number when the date is BC the earlier it happened – 800 BC was a long time *before* 80 BC.

There are other ways of counting years. In the countries where Islam is the main religion, for example, they start counting their years from Muhammad's flight from Mecca. This happened in the year we call AD 622, so in Islamic countries the number of the year is not the same as ours. The Jewish calendar starts back further than the Christian one, and the year that we call AD 2000 will be the Jewish year 5760 and the Islamic year 1420.

One last word is important before we leave the ways historians count years, and that word is **century**. A century is one hundred years. We say that we live in the twentieth century. That means we live in the twentieth set of 100 years after the birth of Christ. However, the date of years in the twentieth century does not start with '20' but with '19'. The year 1966 was not in the nineteenth century, but in the twentieth century. The following diagram should help you see why.

The first two centuries AD.

The year 150 is in the second century because it is in the second set of 100 years after the birth of Christ. The first century was all the years up to 100.

1 What do the abbreviations AD and BC stand for?

2 From which event do Christian countries start counting their years? Why do you think they chose this event?

3 If you had two newspapers for the same day, one from London and one from Mecca (the Islamic holy city), why would they have different dates?

4 What century were the following years in?

  a 1537   b 635   c 1973
  d 1066   e 1215   f 87
  g 1654   h 333 BC i 1111
  j 234

5 Give one year in each of these centuries:

  a twentieth century
  b sixth century
  c fourteenth century
  d ninth century
  e eighteenth century
  f fifteenth century
  g eighth century
  h second century BC
  i first century
  j nineteenth century

6 Julius Caesar first visited Britain in 55 BC. He came back the next year. What was the date then?

7 If someone offered to sell you a Roman coin with the date 72 BC on it, would you buy it? Give a reason for your answer.

A reconstruction of a Stone Age village, which contains some anachronisms.

Anachronism

Historians have to be careful about dividing up time, in just the same way that travellers have to be careful about exactly where they are. Just imagine what would happen if a person from Britain, used to driving on the left, went to France and forgot that people there drove on the right. When historians make the same sort of mistake, and mix things up from the wrong time periods, it is called an **anachronism**. If you are tired in school, your teachers may suspect it is because you were up too late the night before watching television. If in the nineteenth century a child working in a factory was tired, the same explanation would be wrong because television had not been invented in the nineteenth century. It would be an anachronism.

Questions

1 What is an anachronism?

2 How many anachronisms are there in the drawing of a Stone Age village? Draw up a table like the one below to show your answer.

Anachronism	Reason

3 Make up a description of something in the past that has an anachronism in it.

4 Why do you think historians say that anachronisms are wrong? Explain your answer.

Clues

The main task of a historian is to find out what happened in the past and to try to explain why it happened. If you wanted to know about an event in the past, such as the coming of the Spanish Armada, you would look it up in a book. But the historians who write the books cannot find things out in such a simple way. The next six units show you the methods historians use to find out about the past. You will have to use these ideas and skills yourself through the rest of the book.

Many people say that historians work like detectives. Detectives have to gather clues about the crime they are trying to solve, and then work out what the clues mean. Historians gather as much information as they can about the thing they are studying. Then they try to work out what happened by trying to **reconstruct** the event from the clues they have collected. The following exercise should show you how this works.

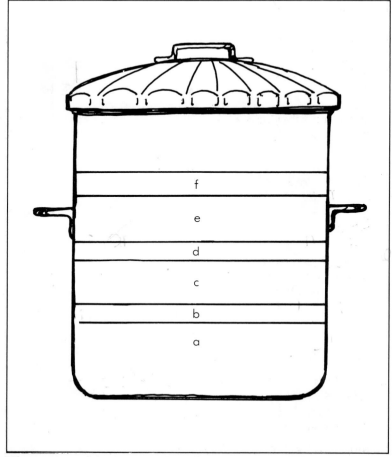

The sections of the dustbin where the various items were found.

Questions

The problem

You work for a secret department of the government catching spies. Your department thinks that the people who live at a certain house might be spies. They went away for several days and then returned. During the time that they were away, some important secrets were stolen from a base in Scotland. The department has got hold of the people's dustbin. You must write a report saying whether or not you think they are dangerous spies by working out as much as you can about the people from what is in their dustbin. Use the investigation department report form to help you.

Table 1: The contents of the dustbin.

Item	Section of the dustbin where it was found
Three opened envelopes all addressed to Mr N. Lewis	a
Empty box of 12 fish fingers	a
Old box of watercolours and painting book	a
Broken children's spade	a
Potato peelings	a, c, e
Empty tub of chocolate ice-cream	a
Empty tins of baby food	a, c, e
Used tea bags	a, c, e
Credit-card slips (see Source A)	a
Empty box of cereal	c
Used razor blade	c
Opened can of baked beans	c
Wrapper for packet of sausages	c
Empty packet of washing powder (see Source B)	c
Two broken hair curlers	c
Radio Times and *TV Times* for week 14–20 September	e
Broken doll	e
The *Daily Mirror*:	
Wednesday 18 September	b
Thursday 19 September	d
Friday 20 September	f

Source A

Some people pay for things with credit cards rather than cash. For every item you buy with a credit card you are given a copy of the slip, which tells the credit-card company how much money you owe. This credit card slip was found in the Lewis family's dustbin.

As well as this slip, there were two others for petrol, both for garages between London and Bournemouth.

One of the credit card slips found in the dustbin.

Source B

The washing-powder box.

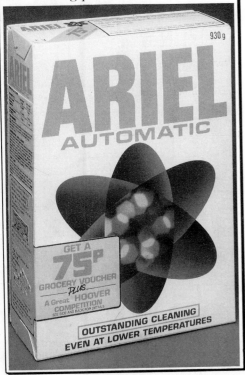

INVESTIGATION DEPARTMENT REPORT FORM

Case: 664/53   Date: Reporting Officer:

Reasons for your answer:

Number of adult men:

Number of adult women:

Number of children:

Names of people
(if known):

List of items they have in
their house:

Car: Yes/No. Type
(if known):

Eating habits:

Other observations
(explanation for time
spent away from home):

Conclusion: The subjects are

   definitely spies.
   probably spies.
   probably not spies.
   definitely not spies.

(delete those that do not apply)

Thinking about Evidence

The year is 1987. The most daring jewel raid in history has just been discovered. Shortly after midnight, a guard patrolling the Tower of London disturbed an armed raider stealing the priceless Crown jewels. The guard was shot dead trying to make an arrest. But there had obviously been a struggle, because police found, on the floor near the body, a wallet dropped by the thief.

The first detectives on the scene were the experienced Inspector Shirley Holmes, and her young rival, Inspector Theo Coaljack. Both realised that solving a crime like this could make them famous. Each was determined to solve the case before the other. Equally, each of them realised that the thief would be trying to leave the country. He had to be stopped.

The two detectives decided to study the contents of the wallet to build up a picture of the owner so that they could circulate a description to airports and docks. They were particularly keen to find out the thief's

- **name**,
- **appearance**,
- **age** and
- **occupation**

to help customs officials checking passports.

They opened the wallet and shared the contents between them. We shall call the documents they found inside the wallet **sources**. Shirley Holmes looked at Sources A, B, then C, while Theo Coaljack looked at Sources D, E, then F. They each began to take notes about the owner of the wallet. When they had finished, they swapped documents, so Shirley could see Sources D, E and F, and Theo Sources A, B and C. They quickly finished their notes, ready to send the description.

'Quickly!' said Shirley to the nearest constable. 'Send this description. We're after a young fair-haired man named Albert Smith. He's 25 to 35 years old, fashionably dressed and he probably works in a surveyor's office.'

'Hang on,' said Theo Coaljack. 'You've got it all wrong. Albert Smith is the name all right, but our man is about 45 to 55 years old and dark haired; in fact, he's probably going bald. My guess is that he's a partner in a firm of surveyors.'

Something was obviously wrong. Both police officers were good detectives. They had studied the same evidence; yet they had come up with very different pictures of the owner of the wallet.

Questions

1 Split into pairs. One person in each pair should become Shirley Holmes and the other Theo Coaljack. The aim is to prove that your detective is right. Remember that each detective is determined to be the one to solve the case.

   Follow their investigation exactly. It is very important that you study the sources in the same order as they did and that you study your first three sources and then take notes before studying the remaining three, just like they did.

2 When you've both finished, try to convince your partner that your solution is right and that your partner is wrong.

3 Once the debate is over, discuss your solutions in class.

   a Which sources provided the strongest evidence for Shirley Holmes?
   b Which sources provided Theo Coaljack with his strongest evidence?
   c Could any of the sources be used as evidence for *both* opinions?

Source A

...otograph. *There is writing on the back, saying 'All my ... Chrissie', and the date 1977.*

Source B

No. 3001	**YOUNG IDEA**		
	Trendsetting fashions for men		
	31 High Street, Greenway		
	VAT No. 310 0002 79		
GOODS		£	p
1 TIE		4	95
	TOTAL	4	95
	Customer's receipt		

A receipt for a tie from a modern fashion shop for men.

Source C

...cond photograph. It also has the date 1977 ...en on the back.

The detectives' problems are similar to the ones that historians have. What *should* happen is that detectives and historians use **sources** as **evidence** to form their **opinions**. However, sometimes the evidence fits more than one opinion, so there's no *right* answer.

But there are times when we don't like to think that we don't know something, or that someone else's opinion is better than ours. Then our opinions become fixed and we start to *twist* the evidence to suit ourselves, to *prove* our opinions. For example, Shirley Holmes believed that the thief was a young person and she ignored the evidence of the ballroom dancing because it didn't suit her opinion. She might have become angry when Theo Coaljack pointed out that young men rarely go ballroom dancing these days. But on the other hand, Theo probably conveniently overlooked the tie from the fashion shop, because it didn't suit his theory.

Did you get angry or twist the evidence?

Source D

```
GREENWAY MUSIC SHOPS
9 410 00 RECORD 5.95



SUBTOTAL 5.95
   TOTAL 5.95

PLEASE RETAIN
YOUR RECEIPT AS
PROOF OF PURCHASE
```

...ceipt for a long-playing ...d.

Source E

Brown, Smith and Jones

Registered Chartered Surveyors

A. Smith FRICS

A printed business card.

Source F

Greenway Ballroom
Dancing Club

Membersnip card no: 0721

Member's signature

Albert Smith

A membership card for a ballroom dancing club.

Primary and Secondary Sources

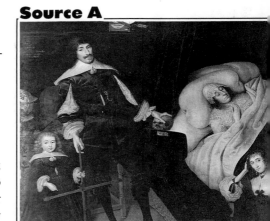

A seventeenth-century nobleman and his fam... painted in about 1625.

The main differences between the way detectives work and the way historians work are the events they try to explain and the evidence they work with. Detectives look for witnesses and go and question them. In history this is usually not possible. You cannot find any survivors from the battle of Hastings to ask them why they thought that the Saxons lost.

Instead, historians have to collect their information from various sources, and do the best they can with what they have managed to collect. The big problem is that the sources may not tell them what they want to know. A detective could go back and ask the witness more questions, but the historian is stuck with whatever the source says.

Think back to the story about the Lewis family in History 1.4. If the investigator had wanted to find out more about the family he or she could have done. He or she could have thought that the family did not really go to Bournemouth, but instead sent people to pretend they were the Lewises. He or she could check this by questioning people in the hotel, and perhaps by showing them photographs of the real Lewises. A historian studying a problem that happened a long time ago cannot do this.

Because historians have only a limited number of sources to work from, they have to be very careful about how they use the sources that they do have. The sources that historians use can be divided into two main types, called **primary** and **secondary**.

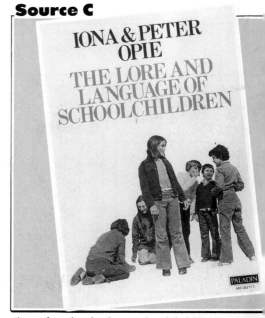

Children's Games painted by the artist Brueg... in 1559.

Primary sources

A primary source is something that comes from the time that the historian is studying. If a historian is studying the First World War, then letters and diaries written by soldiers, the uniforms they wore and the weapons that they used are all primary sources. If a soldier who fought in the trenches wrote about his memories of the war a long time after the war had finished, it would still be a primary source.

Secondary sources

Secondary sources are sources which do not come from the time that the historian is studying. These sources have got their information from other sources. Books about the First World War by historians, or school textbooks about the First World War, are examples of secondary sources.

A modern book about schoolchildren in the la... 1970s.

Source D

A book about fashion, 1200–1980.

Source E

A book about children in England from Tudor times to the eighteenth century.

Source F

School pupil dressed up in historical costume.

See question 4 below on Sources A – F.

Activity

Are the following sources primary or secondary?

a Canterbury Cathedral
b *Britain since 1700* by R.J. Cootes (Longman 1968)
c *Report on the Excavations at Canterbury Castle* (1982) by Paul Bennett
d *The Six Wives of Henry VIII* (film on television)
e Letters from Lord Nelson to Lady Hamilton
f A Victorian photo of the fields where your school was built
g The text of a speech by Oliver Cromwell
h The Black Prince's armour
i *Ivanhoe* by Sir Walter Scott (a historical novel)
j *The Times*, 5 August 1914 (the day after the First World War broke out)

You may have found this exercise difficult because you do not know what you are supposed to be studying. In fact, you cannot really decide whether a source is primary or secondary until you know what it is that you are trying to find out about. Take example **b** from the exercise. If you want to know about life in Britain after 1700 the book will be a secondary source. However, if a historian in the future wanted to know about how people were taught in schools in the 1980s then the book by Cootes would be a primary source, because it is a textbook used in schools in the 1980s.

Questions

Section A

1 Why is it harder for a historian to use sources than for a detective?

2 Write a definition of a primary source, and give an example.

3 Write a definition of a secondary source, and give an example.

Section B

4 You are a historian who is going to write three books: one about the way people have dressed, called *Changing Fashion*; one about childhood, called *Children from 1066 to the Present Day*; and one called *Schools in the Last Ten Years*. For each of these books Sources A – F might be primary (P), secondary (S) or no real use (NU). Draw up a table like the one below, and then work out what type of source each would be for each book.

	Changing Fashion	Children from 1066 to the Present Day	Schools in the Last Ten Years
Source A			
Source B			

5 Make a list of the ten best primary sources you can think of for someone who is going to write a history of your school. Explain why you think each source will be a good one.

6 Give your own example of a source that can be both primary and secondary. Explain why it could be both.

Different Types of Sources

W hen people think of the sources that historians use they tend to think of old manuscripts and other documents. In fact, historians will use anything that has survived from the past. One of the most famous historical finds in recent years has been the Tudor warship the *Mary Rose*. Not one written document has survived in the ship, but from the ship historians have learnt all sorts of things – from some of the medical treatments that were used at the time to what games the sailors played in their spare time.

The diagram below shows the various sources that a historian could use.

The various sources used by historians.

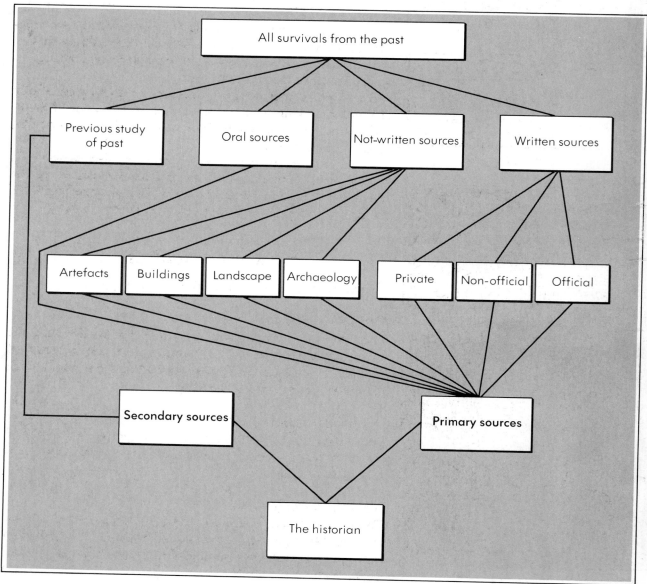

Source A

Sumerian clay tablet, BC 3500.

Source B

Egyptian hieroglyphics, BC 700.

Source C

Mayan hieroglyphics, 761 AD.

The differences between primary and secondary sources were explained in the last chapter. The 'previous study of the past', which is in the box leading to secondary sources in the diagram showing the various sources used by historians, could be either the study of primary sources, or the study of earlier secondary sources, or both.

In some cases, when they are studying fairly recent events, historians can talk to people who were there at the time. This is not done very often because most history is written about events too long ago for there to be anyone left alive.

The most obvious division between types of primary source is between those sources which are written and those which are not written.

Activity

Are Sources A, B and C examples of written or not-written sources?

Source A is a clay tablet made by people called Sumerians about 3500 BC. It tells of a war and of a man's illness, and is written in **cuneiform**, a system of writing using a triangular wedge to make marks in wet clay.

B is also a written source. It describes the conquest of part of Egypt by a king from Nubia. It was written about 700 BC, and is written in **hieroglyphics**, a type of picture-writing used in Ancient Egypt.

C is also a written source, and is also written in hieroglyphics, but this time the picture-writing is by the Maya, who lived in South America. The written text is on the right-hand side, and the pillar was put up in AD 761.

Written sources

Written sources can be divided into three types:

Official documents
These are any written sources which are to do with the government or the law. Examples are the records of Parliament, income tax forms, school registers, and Source C, which was set up by the king.

Private documents
These have to do with one particular person. Letters and diaries are good examples. Source A is also an example, as it was a letter.

Non-official documents
These include all documents that are neither official nor private. Newspapers, adverts and Source B, which is a history of recent events, are all examples of non-official documents.

Sources that are not written

To describe all the sorts of non-written documents we need four categories:

Archaeology

This is the study of remains that are under the earth and have to be excavated. Probably the most famous example is Pompeii, the Roman city which was buried by a volcano and which has been uncovered in the last two hundred years by archaeologists.

The landscape

The land itself holds many clues about life in the past. Most things which happen to the soil leave marks that can be spotted. In Source D you can see the marks that have been left by a Roman fort.

Buildings

Those buildings which survive are very useful. The earliest building in Britain is a prehistoric bridge; and as you get later in time, so more buildings have survived.

Artefacts

These are all those things made by people. There are many different sources of this type: from paintings and sculpture to tools and clothes.

Questions

Section A

1 Copy the diagram of the sources used by historians (see page 14) into your book.

2 Write a sentence describing each of the types of primary source. Give an example for each type of a source which could be used by a historian studying life at your school today.

Section B

3 Look at sources E – K. If a historian was studying the English Civil War which type would each of the sources be? Give reasons for your answer.

Source E: *Aerial view of a battlefield in the English Civil War.* ▶

Source F: *Extract from the burial register of Cropredy Church, 1644. The register reads: 'Five soldiers buried the last day of June. Edward Webb, major of the King's horse, was buried the sixth day of July.'* ▶

Source G: *Cropredy Bridge in the nineteenth century.* ▶

Source D

The Roman fort that stood on this site has long since disappeared, but it has left marks on the landscape that can be seen clearly from the air.

Source E

Source F

Source G

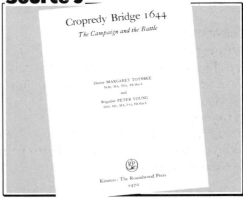

Source H

Source H: *Page from the 'Happy Progresse' by Sir Edward Walker. This page describes the Royalist order of march before the Battle of Cropredy Bridge in June 1644.*

Source I: *Title page of a book about the Battle of Cropredy Bridge published in 1644.*

Source J: *Title page of a book about the Battle of Cropredy Bridge published in 1970.*

Source I

18

An Exact and full

RELATION
OF THE LAST

FIGHT,

Between the KINGS Forces
and Sir WILLIAM WALLER.

Sent in a Letter from an Officer
in the Army to his friend in *London*.

Printed to prevent mis-information.

LONDON
Printed for *Ben. Allen*, in Popes-Head-Alley.
July 3. 1 6 4 4.

Source J

Cropredy Bridge 1644
The Campaign and the Battle

Doctor MARGARET TOYNBEE
Ph.D., MA, FSA, FR Hist S

and

Brigadier PETER YOUNG
DSO, MC, MA, FSA, FR Hist S

Kineton: The Roundwood Press
1970

Source K

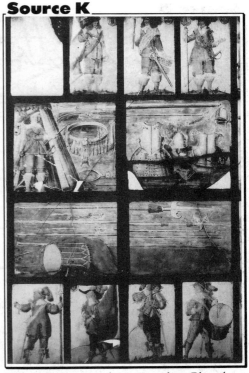

Painted glass window, Farndon Church.

Photographs as Sources

Photographs give us glimpses of the past as it appeared when they were taken, which makes them vivid historical sources. You may have heard the phrase, 'The camera does not lie,' which – if it is true – makes photographs very special historical sources indeed. This unit looks at photographs as historical sources. Do historians need special techniques to use them? Are they always reliable?

Activity

Study Source A carefully. What could a historian say, having looked at the photograph?

Source A

Having thought carefully about Source A you can probably say more about it now than you could when you first looked at it. So photographs are the same as any other source a historian might use – they have to be studied carefully and interpreted.

All photographs are taken with a purpose. This is clear in Source A where the people are posing for the photograph and have been carefully arranged by the photographer. Source A records an important event in the life of a family. A historian does not have to have the same purpose in order to find the photograph useful.

Activity

How many ways could a historian use the photograph in Source A?

The importance of knowing why a photograph was taken is clear when we look at Source B. In the 1870s there were thought to be about 30,000 homeless children sleeping rough in London and getting money for food in any way they could. Selling matches on street corners was one way of making a little money.

Source B

Katie Smith, a London matchseller, in about 1874.

Activities

1 Do you think Katie Smith (Source B) would have had three good meals a day and a warm bed at night?

2 Does Source B suggest that something needed to be done to look after London's homeless children?

3 Does Source B suggest children were not looked after as well in the 1870s as they are now?

4 Why do you think the photograph of Katie Smith was taken?

You cannot answer question 4 about Source B very well without having some extra information. The photograph was taken by the photographic unit of Dr Barnardo's Homes. The charity rescued homeless children from the streets and provided them with a home, education and training for a job. Thomas Barnardo raised the money to run his homes from gifts from the general public. To encourage the public to give money he ran what we would call an advertising campaign. Another charity worker at the time wrote of his methods:

'Barnardo's method is to take [photographs of] the children as they are supposed to enter the home, and then after they have been at the home for some time. He is not satisfied with taking the children as they really are, but he tears their clothes to make them appear worse than they really are. They are also taken in purely fictional positions.'

Barnardo was taken to court for his 'advertising' methods. He was found guilty. Katie Smith was a child in one of Barnardo's homes, but she had never been a match seller, and she had dressed up in rags and posed specially for the picture.

Activity

Think back to your answers to the questions about Source B. Which answers would you now want to change?

Questions

1 Source A does not have a caption. Write a caption for it and explain why you think your caption is a good one.

2 Look at the caption to Source B. Either write a new caption for it or keep the existing caption. Whichever you choose, explain why.

3 Copy these statements into your book and then explain whether you agree with them or not:

a Photographs never lie.
b A photograph is only as reliable as its caption.

19

How Historians Use Sources

One of the things that historians have to be very careful about is whether they can trust what their sources say. They want to know if the source is **reliable**. Both primary and secondary sources can be reliable or unreliable. It does not make any difference which type of source it is. However, historians do need to know which type of source they are using because they check to see whether or not primary and secondary sources are reliable in different ways.

To check a primary source, the historian will be most concerned with two things. First, did the person who wrote it actually know what they were talking about? You could write something about what it felt like to orbit the Earth in the Space Shuttle, but it would not be reliable because you would have to imagine what it would feel like.

The second check has to do with the ideas of the person who wrote the source. Some people may not tell the truth because of the way they feel about things. A good example of this can often be found after football matches. Supporters of the two teams sometimes give completely different accounts of the game.

Working out whether a source is reliable or not is just one of the jobs that historians need to do with their sources. Sources that are not written documents often need to be **interpreted**. The historian has to work out what the source is saying.

Activity

What can you learn about the ancient Greeks from the wine jar in Source A?

You should have thought of things to do with Greek clothes, arms and armour and perhaps pottery. But did you work out anything about their farming, their knowledge of geography and the methods of transport available at the time?

When historians use sources to back up their statements we call the sources **evidence**. For example, a historian could make the following statement: 'Ancient Greek farmers grew grapes.' The picture of the wine jar could be used as evidence to support this statement, because wine is made from grapes.

Questions

Section A

1 Each of the following statements is either true or false. Copy out each statement and write a sentence explaining whether the statement is true or false.

   a A historian can only trust certain sources.
   b All primary sources must be reliable.
   c A primary source must be reliable if the person was actually there when the event happened.
   d Secondary sources are never reliable.
   e A source becomes evidence only when a historian uses it to prove something.

Section B

2 Explain how Source A can be used as evidence to support the following statements:

   a The ancient Greeks knew how to make wine.
   b The ancient Greeks used armour to protect their bodies.
   c The ancient Greeks had highly developed skills in painting.
   d The ancient Greeks knew how to write.
   e The ancient Greeks had some contact with Africa.

3 Make up a statement of your own about the Greeks and explain how the photo of the wine jar can be used as evidence to support it.

4 Using Source B as evidence, what can you say about life in Ur? Make a list of at least ten statements, and in each case explain how you have been able to work out your statement.

Source A

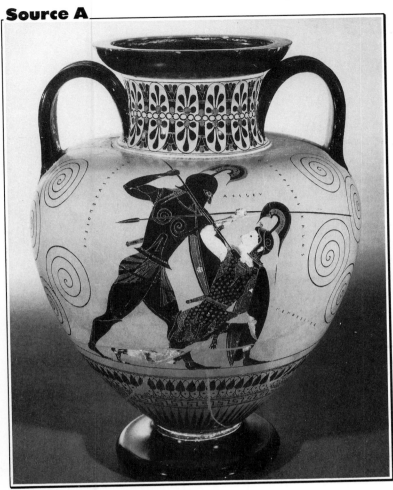

An ancient Greek wine jar.

Source B

*'The Standard of Ur.' A decorated panel made with bitumen inlaid
with stones. This was found in the ruins of the city of Ur in Iraq and
was made about 2000 BC.*

Why did the Mary Rose Sink?

To finish this part of the book we will look at one problem historians have tried to solve. We will see how the skills you have learnt so far can help you to come up with your own solution to the problem.

Background information

In 1545 a French fleet attacked the English fleet in the Solent, the stretch of water between the Isle of Wight and the mainland. The weather was not good for sailing ships; there was not enough wind. The French had some galleys (ships which were rowed by oarsmen), and these came close enough to the English ships to shoot at them. When the wind was strong enough, some English ships sailed towards the French. At about this time the *Mary Rose* sank. Was the *Mary Rose* sunk by French cannon-fire, or was there some other reason?

Source B

A picture of the battle painted soon afterwards, showing the sinking of the Mary Rose. *You can see the masts of the* Mary Rose *sticking up out of the water just above Southsea Castle in the centre. The coast of the Isle of Wight is on the left.*

The only contemporary picture of the Mary Rose.

Source A

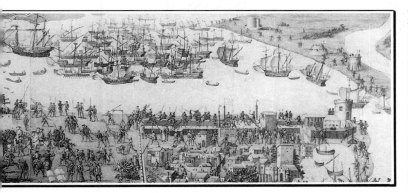

The problem

Which of these theories is most likely to be true?

a The French sank the *Mary Rose* by cannon-fire.

b The *Mary Rose* tilted over, water came in through the gunports, and it sank.

Answering the following questions should help you make up your mind:

1 By themselves do Sources A and B help you solve the problem?

2 Is there any reason why Source C may not be reliable?

3 Is there any reason why Source D may not be reliable?

4 Do Sources C and D agree about anything?

5 Does Source A support the version of either Source C or Source D?

6 What advantages will Source E have for the historian?

7 Does Source E support theory A?

8 Does Source E support theory B?

9 Supporting your answer with as much evidence as you can, say what you think happened to the *Mary Rose*.

10 Do you think your answer is definitely true or probably true? Give reasons for your answer.

Source C

'Our galleys [caused] great damage to the English, who could not move because there was no wind, so they could not avoid our cannon and hardly a shot missed them. Fortune favoured our fleet in this manner for above an hour, during which time the *Mary Rose* was sunk by our cannon, and of 500 or 600 men which were on board only 35 escaped.'

From an account by D'Annebault, the French commander.

Source D

'Sir George Carew commanded every man to take his place, and the sails to be hoist, but the same was no sooner done than the *Mary Rose* began to lean over to one side. [The captain of another ship] passing by the *Mary Rose* called out to Sir George Carew asking what was wrong. He answered he had a sort of knaves he could not rule [the crew would not obey him] and it was not long after that the *Mary Rose*, leaning more and more, was drowned. Of the 700 men who were in her, very few escaped.'

From an account by an English captain present at the battle.

Source E

Between 1967 and 1983 the wreck of the *Mary Rose* was found and excavated by underwater archaeologists. Two of their findings are useful to us:

1 The site of the wreck.
2 The gunports.

When the archaeologists got down to the side of the ship they found evidence that suggested that the gunports had been fixed open.

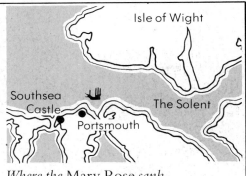

Where the Mary Rose *sank.*

Julius Caesar's Invasions: the Background

One morning in August 55 BC, a large group of Britons stood on the cliffs near Dover. They were looking out to sea, prepared for war. Their faces were painted blue with woad (a form of war-paint). They were armed with swords and spears, and some were on horseback or in chariots. A fleet of about one hundred ships appeared, carrying 12,000 first-rate troops led by Julius Caesar, the all-conquering Roman general.

The first Roman invasion of Britain was about to begin. Who were those Britons? Who were Julius Caesar and the Romans? Why was Caesar invading?

Who were the Britons?

The people who lived in Britain had come in large numbers from central Europe and from what is now France. Many thousands of these people, known as **Celts,** had crossed the English Channel during the last six hundred years. They were divided into small tribal groups and were ruled by tribal kings.

The Britons looked different from the Romans. They were mostly taller, with blond hair and blue eyes, and they dressed in rough tunics, cloaks and boots. Since most of lowland Britain was at this time covered in thick forests, people lived in small villages in the upland areas like the South Downs and the Chiltern and Cotswold hills. The Celts had developed the use of iron, horses and chariots. Their craftspeople used the potter's wheel. They minted metal coins and built large, impressive hill-forts, protected by earth banks.

Caesar's landings.

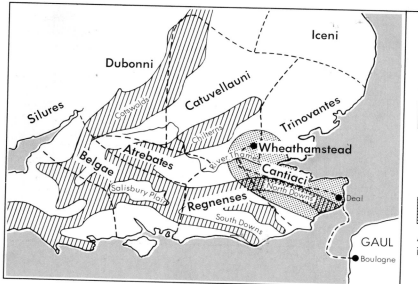

Areas of chalk or limestone uplands occupied by Celtic settlements.

Tribal boundaries changed rapidly at this time, but this is an idea of the location of the Celtic tribes.

Area invaded by Caesar in 55 and 54 BC

Source A

A Roman ship at the time of the invasions.

The Celts were farmers, producing corn and wool from the fields and raising horses. They also mined tin, lead, silver, copper and gold, and traded with European merchants from the Continent.

Who was Julius Caesar?

The strong and growing empire of Rome was hard to rule. Power was in the hands of army generals like Julius Caesar and his rival, Pompey. Both generals led successful and loyal armies. Caesar hoped to increase his power by conquering more land for Rome. He had conquered most of the land of Gaul (now called France). By 55 BC his army had reached the English Channel.

Why did Caesar invade Britain?

During his battles, Caesar had seen that the Gauls were helped by the Britons. Caesar may have wanted revenge against the Britons. He may also have wanted to make his control of Gaul stronger by defeating the Britons. Britain was rich in grain and metals, and Caesar could demand money or capture prisoners and sell them as slaves.

Fortunately for Caesar, British tribes often fought among themselves. Some Britons had asked the Romans to invade and help them against their enemies.

It was late summer, and the good weather needed for campaigning was running out. 'Even if there were not time for a campaign that season,' wrote Caesar, 'it would be of great advantage to visit the island to see what the inhabitants were like.' Another victory would help his reputation in Rome.

Questions

Section A

1 Make a list of the different tribes in southern England, using the map.

2 List the things you know about the Britons which show they were not simple savages.

3 Julius Caesar fought a long campaign in Gaul:

  a Why do you think he needed ships like the one in Source A to help him?
  b Do you think Source A is a true picture of one of the ships Caesar used?

Section B

4 Three possible causes of Caesar's invasion of Britain are given in points a, b and c. Copy them into your book. Can you find any more?

  a Caesar would get more fame and glory from an invasion.
  b Some Britons had asked for help against their hostile neighbours.
  c Caesar could get grain and precious metals for Rome.

5 Now write out the list again in order of importance. Write down the reason for the invasion which you think was the main one first, and so on until you write the one least important last.

6 Not all the causes of Caesar's invasion of Britain were equally important. Some were very important causes and some were not important at all — almost excuses for invading rather than reasons. From your list of possible causes, write down one that you think was an important cause, and one that you think was just an excuse. Explain your answer.

25

Julius Caesar's Invasion: the Landings

The first landing

In 55 BC Julius Caesar decided to invade Britain with two legions, the Seventh and the Tenth. Each Roman legion had about 5,500 soldiers in it. A supporting fleet carrying supplies and cavalry would follow soon afterwards. When his ships arrived off the Kent coast, and he saw the waiting Britons on the cliff ready to hurl their spears down on his troops, Caesar decided to sail along the coast to a safer landing place.

He had been told that Richborough harbour would be suitable, but he could not find it. Caesar landed at a beach near Deal, still watched by the Britons. However, his boats ran aground some yards from the beach and the Romans were sitting targets for the British spears – read Source A which explains how Caesar's troops overcame these problems.

Caesar's troops had won their first victory in Britain. The Romans could have pressed on, but Caesar decided that his small army could be attacked by the Britons in their horse-drawn chariots. So he ordered his men to build a fortified camp, and waited for his supplies and cavalry.

Four days later there was a storm. Heavy rain and winds dashed the shore. The tide swept high up the beaches. Caesar was taken by surprise. Several of the Roman ships were wrecked, the supplies and cavalry were delayed, and the Britons' chariots began to attack the camp. After beating off the attack, Caesar held negotiations – talks – with the Britons. He kept quiet about his army's difficulties and asked for money and hostages in exchange for leaving the Britons alone. The Britons agreed, and Caesar sailed back to Gaul. He sent reports to Rome of his discoveries and his victories, saying little about his hurried departure.

The second landing

In the following year, 54 BC, Caesar returned. This time his force was better prepared. The Romans took about 800 ships and five legions with cavalry, in all more than 30,000 men.

Source A

'The soldiers, unfamiliar with the ground and with their hands full, had to jump down from the ships, get a footing in the waves, and fight. The enemy, standing on dry land, threw spears and galloped their horses into the sea. This frightened our soldiers until the standard-bearer shouted, "Jump down, comrades, unless you want to lose our Eagle." He leapt from the boat and advanced towards the enemy. When they saw this, the soldiers jumped from the boat and followed him. Both sides fought hard. Caesar loaded small fast boats with troops to be sent to any point where his men were in trouble. Once the soldiers had got a foothold on the beach they charged the enemy and put them to flight.'

From Julius Caesar, 'The Conquest of Gaul', c. 52 BC, translated by S.A. Handford (Penguin, 1982).

Source C

A Celtic helmet with neck flap.

Source B

A Celtic short sword.

The newly designed Roman ships could now sail closer to the beach. Caesar set sail earlier than he had the year before, on 6 July, and again landed near Deal.

This time there was practically no opposition from the Britons. The Roman legions marched inland. But news then arrived that some of the ships had been lost and damaged in a storm, and Caesar ordered a retreat to the coast. Repairs cost ten days before the army again went inland.

The most powerful tribe among the Britons was the **Catuvellauni**, under their king, Cassivellaunus. The Catuvellauni wisely avoided a full-scale battle, and raided the Roman columns with swift chariot attacks instead. The Romans struck north to Cassivellaunus's base at Wheathampstead. If the British tribes had banded together they could have fought off the invaders, but some tribes hated the Catuvellauni. They did nothing, and this allowed Caesar to capture Wheathampstead. Even a surprise attack by another tribe, the Cantiaci, on Caesar's base in Kent could not unsettle the Romans. They looked secure.

However, Caesar decided to leave. He may have felt he had gained enough glory from his victories. Possibly he worried that he hadn't enough troops or that future storms could again wreck his fleet. He had also heard rumours of trouble in Gaul. Roman bases there were short of manpower, because of the number of soldiers taken to invade Britain. Caesar again took hostages and money, and sailed back to Gaul. It would be nearly one hundred years before the Romans conquered Britain.

Source D

...eltic shield.

Source E

A Roman legionary with a variety of weapons.

Questions

Section A

1 Write a list of five reasons why Caesar's invasion of 55 BC went less well than he had hoped. Use the title '55 BC: Causes of Failure'.

2 Write a list of the reasons why Caesar's second invasion went better than the first. Use the title '54 BC: Causes of Success'.

3 Using Sources A – E, which side do you think was better equipped and better organised in the fighting – the Romans or the Britons? Give reasons for your answer.

Section B

4 Here is a list of phrases called 'heads' and 'tails' which go together to make sentences. Write out the sentences, matching each head with its tail. Each sentence has a cause and an effect: write (C) next to the cause and (E) next to the effect.

Heads	Tails
a Caesar's ships ran aground in deep water	because he had too few men.
b Caesar had no hope of conquering Britain in 55 BC	so the Roman army was never seriously in danger.
c The Britons failed to combine forces	and his soldiers were therefore at a disadvantage.

5 Julius Caesar gained great fame and honour in Rome from his victories in Britain, even though he failed to conquer the country.

a Some of the things that happened were beyond his control. Find one cause of Caesar's failure to conquer Britain which was beyond his control – it was due to bad luck. Explain why you have chosen it.

b Some of the events were influenced by Caesar and his men. Find one cause of Caesar's success in battle which was the result of his or his army's actions. Explain why you have chosen it.

Everyday Life in Rome

This unit will help you build up a picture of everyday life in Ancient Rome at the time of Caesar's invasions.

But remember that the life of a Roman person depended on whether they were rich, poor or a slave, and on their sex and their age. Life in Ancient Rome was not the same in 200 BC as it was in AD 200, and living conditions were different in Roman Gaul, Roman Africa and Rome itself. So there were many variations to the details of life described below.

Clothes

Roman men and women wore a short-sleeved tunic, tied at the waist. These were usually knee-length for men, ankle-length for women. Poor people, workmen and slaves would wear these tunics in the street, but the wealthy would always wear a **toga** over their tunic. This was a large piece of cloth wrapped around the body and draped over one shoulder. It was the symbol of the Roman citizen, a sign of status. Cloaks would be worn in cold weather, when leather shoes replaced open sandals. Slaves usually went barefoot.

Eating

Breakfast was usually bread, cheese and a little wine or water. Lunch was a bigger meal of cold meat, vegetables and fruit, again with bread and wine or water. The main meal was dinner in the early evening, perhaps at five o'clock. There would be several courses. Beef, mutton and pork were the most common meats eaten, but rich people treated their guests to more exotic meats, including flamingoes, peacocks, storks, doves and dormice.

Spoons and knives were used, but forks were not, because most eating was done with the fingers. Men usually lay on their side on a couch and helped themselves to food from a low central table; women and children often sat on upright chairs. For many Roman families, the meal would be served by slaves.

Family life

The Roman wife shared her husband's social position outside the home and his authority inside it. Men were very much in control of their children, who were expected to be loyally obedient to their father even when they were grown up. This sense of duty helped the Roman army control its soldiers. Fathers found husbands and wives for their children during their teens. Girls could marry at twelve, boys at fourteen.

Source A

A carving showing a Roman shop.

Source B

A carving showing a shop selling cutlery.

Questions

Section A

1 What is being sold in the shop in Source A?

2 What is the man in Source A wearing?

3 Which figure is the customer and which one the tradesman in Source B? Explain your answer.

4 Which figures in Source C are men and which ones are women? Explain your answer.

5 Who are the figures on the left of Source C and what are they doing?

6 a Describe the typical hair-style of Roman men.
  b Were Roman men usually clean-shaven or bearded?

7 Copy out the following paragraph, choosing the best alternative from the brackets.

The (mother/father) was the dominant person in the Roman family. At family meals, (men/women) lay on couches while (men/women) and (children/slaves) sat in upright chairs. There would be a (great variety/small selection) of meats, and the main meal was (at midday/in the evening). All classes in Roman society wore (togas/tunics), but wealthier citizens wore a (toga/belt) over it. Roman men were usually (bare-headed/hatted) and (clean-shaven/bearded).

Section B

8 How would Roman citizens have felt about:

  a being in the streets without their toga or sandals?
  b being offered beef and mutton by their host at dinner?
  c two teenagers who fell in love and wanted to marry?

  Explain each answer.

urce C

...ving showing Romans eating a meal.

Housing and Health in Rome

By AD 200 the city of Rome contained about 1.2 million people. They needed a large number of buildings – shops, temples, theatres and public baths. But most of all they needed homes.

Most people in Rome lived in blocks of flats, five or six storeys high, in which they rented one or two rooms. They were furnished with a few bare stools and tables and no beds at all; people usually slept on mats and blankets. These flats, called **insulae**, had windows, but no glass – just wooden shutters. There was no water supply or plumbing above the ground floor. Sewage was disposed of through the windows – see Source A.

Outside the blocks of flats the streets were narrow and crowded, often unpaved, unlit and filthy with rubbish and sewage. According to the writer Juvenal, it could be dangerous to be out at night.

Richer citizens lived in a one- or two-storey house, called a **domus**, built of brick or stone and whitewashed at the front. These homes were pleasant, set back from the roads. They had entrance areas or shops at the front to cut down the noise from the street. Inside, rooms faced on to courtyards with gardens and sometimes fountains. Some rooms might be heated by an under-floor hot air system called a **hypocaust**. Only about one in twenty of the inhabitants of Rome lived in such houses.

Grander still was the country house, or **villa**, outside the city. The remains of many villas, with their splendid mosaic floors, have survived because they were not built upon over the centuries. But these homes were not typical of the average Roman citizen's dwelling.

Apart from housing, the huge population of Rome caused many other problems. The amount of traffic on the narrow roads became so great that for many years carts were banned except at night. How to get fresh water and what to do with sewage were also problems. Rome came to have the best water supply and sewerage system of any city in the ancient world. Romans recognized the importance of fresh water for healthy living, and their public baths became regular meeting-places for the middle and upper classes.

We can read descriptions of the Roman fountains, baths, sewers and aqueducts written at the time. We can also study their remains. Look at Sources C – G about **public health** in Roman times.

Source A

'Along your way each open window may be a death trap. So hope and pray, you poor man, that the housewives drop nothing worse on your head than a bedpan full of slops.'

From Juvenal, 'Satires'.

Source B

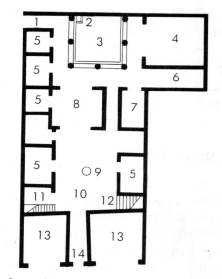

1 Second Entrance
2 Shrine to the household gods
3 Courtyard or garden
4 Dining room
5 Summer bedrooms
    (bedrooms used in winter on upper floor)
6 Kitchen
7 Living room
8 Study
9 Basin to collect rainwater
10 Entrance hall (atrium)
11 Servants' stairs
12 Stairs to upper floor
13 Shops (run by the owner of the house)
14 Entrance

A plan of the house of the Tragic Poet at Pompeii.

Source C

'My job concerns the health of the city, so this task has always been handled by the most important of men. For 441 years Romans were satisfied to use water from the Tiber and nearby springs and wells. Now, nine aqueducts bring water to the city. Compare such building works (aqueducts, baths and sewers) with the idle Pyramids and useless though famous buildings of the Greeks.'

From Julius Frontinus, 'The Aqueducts of Rome', c.AD 97 (Frontinus was in charge of Rome's water supply).

Source D

'Water is brought to the city in such quantities through aqueducts that is like a river flowing through the city.'

From Strobo, 'Geography', first century BC (Strobo was a Greek geographer).

Source F

'Public baths were an essential part of town planning. If the Britons were to become Romans they had to adopt a liking for a daily bath.... Though drainage was an important feature of Roman towns [in Britain], only Lincoln is known to have had a planned sewerage system.'

From Anthony Birley, 'Life in Roman Britain', 1964.

Source G

'Men still admire the city sewers. They were built 700 years ago by Tarquinus and they are still undamaged. He made the tunnels big enough for a waggon to pass through.'

From Pliny, 'Natural History', first century AD.

Source E

Lavatories in the forum baths at Ostia.

Questions

Section A

1 Why was house-building important in Rome?

2 Draw a plan of the house of the Tragic Poet (Source B) in your book. Give your drawing a key explaining which of the numbers go with the following labels:
   Courtyard   Shops   Entrance   Living-room or bedroom

3 Would the house in Source B be the sort of home most Roman people lived in? Explain your answer.

4 Make a list of as many differences as you can between the homes of the rich and those of the poor.

Section B

5 Does Source C show that the Romans looked after the health of their citizens?

6 What do you know about Frontinus (Source C) that makes you think he might be a reliable source?

7 Is there any reason to think that Frontinus could be an unreliable source?

8 Re-read all the sources. Does each of the other sources agree or disagree with Frontinus? Write a sentence explaining your answer for each source.

9 Do you agree that because we have lots of written evidence about Roman water supply and sewers we do not need to bother to excavate the remains of the Roman cities to find out about them?

Slavery and the Games

A million or more people lived in Ancient Rome in the third century AD. Some were wealthy generals, senators and magistrates; many were middle-class merchants, business people, craft workers and shopkeepers; but the majority were poor. The biggest group of all was the **slaves**, workers who were the property of their owners.

People could become slaves in many different ways: by being in debt, as punishment for certain crimes, or by being captured in wars. Some poor parents even sold their children as slaves, although this was against the law. Slaves' children became the slaves of their parents' owners.

House slaves lived with the family who owned them. They were usually fairly treated, sometimes becoming almost one of the family. By about AD 300 most middle-class Roman households had several house slaves. The famous writer Pliny the Younger had 500 slaves, and the Emperor may have had 20,000 or more. Flogging a slave to death was not illegal. There were many cases of cruel treatment, although the spread of Christianity probably led to improvements.

The Romans mostly saw nothing wrong with slavery. The Greek writer Aristotle had taught that few people were good enough to be trusted with complete freedom. Slavery saved the slave from evil temptations and idleness and saved the owner unnecessary work. It was thought that slavery was the result of normal bad luck and not a matter of shame. Slaves could become clerks, teachers, bank managers and bailiffs if they were clever, and could even buy their freedom. The only area of Roman life that they were banned from was the army.

Another use for slaves was in **entertainment**. Most actors

Source A

The small theatre at Pompeii.

Source B

The amphitheatre at Pompeii.

were slaves; their performances took place in the open-air or small covered theatres.

The great amphitheatres like the Colosseum in Rome were for 'the games' rather than plays. Rich private individuals or the government would arrange entertainments, often on one of Rome's 120 public holidays each year. The games were held first to please the gods, but later they became weekly events. Some of the amphitheatres were huge; the Circus Maximus could seat 150,000 people.

These entertainments might include chariot races, fights between gladiators and even mock sea-battles in a flooded arena. The chariots usually had four horses, and between four and twelve chariots would race around a narrow oval circuit with dangerous tight turns at either end. Chariots often collided and crashed; the charioteers were sometimes killed.

Other games would involve fights to the death between men or between animals and men. The **gladiators**, like the charioteers, were slaves; and the crowds at the fights, like those at the racing, loved the combination of spectacle, bloodshed and skill. Gladiator fights were common for more than five hundred years in Rome, from about 260 BC onwards. Sometimes huge numbers died. For the one-thousandth anniversary of the founding of Rome, 2,000 gladiators were billed to die in fights between men on horseback, or in armour, or with tridents and nets, or with swords and shields. Successful gladiators would turn to the Emperor or to the organiser of the games to get the 'thumbs up' or 'thumbs down' signal. Depending on this, they killed or spared the life of the fighter they had beaten.

Men also fought bulls, bears, lions and other wild beasts. The practice of throwing Christians and others unarmed to the wild animals was common, although during only one period of the Roman Empire. As more and more Romans became Christians, the games were made less blood-thirsty. But the games lasted until the end of the Empire.

Questions

Section A

1 Write a list of the different ways in which people could become slaves.

2 List the jobs that slaves might have done.

3 Which do you think was more popular, the theatre or the games? Give reasons for your answer.

4 Make up a poster which could have been used to advertise the games. Make sure it includes descriptions of the things that would be happening.

Section B

5 Roman slaves were allowed to buy their freedom. Many slaves who had enough money to buy their freedom chose not to. Does this mean these slaves must have been stupid?

6 'The Roman amphitheatres and the games that were put on in them show that the Romans were uncivilised barbarians?' Do you agree? Give reasons for your answer.

Source C

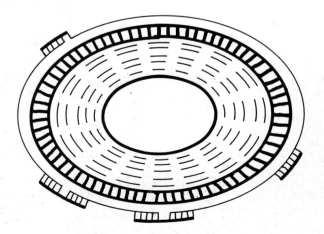

Scale plans of the small theatre and the amphitheatre at Pompeii.

The Religions of the Romans

The Romans knew that they could not control every part of their lives. Storms, floods, drought and illness could all bring disaster. Like many other early civilisations, they began to believe that powerful spirits or gods controlled the world around them. These beings lived in the earth, the sky, the forests and the rivers. To get good luck, the Romans tried to please these spirits and gods with gifts and prayers.

Household spirits

Every Roman household honoured spirits of the house, or **Lares**. These included Vesta, the spirit of the hearth, and Janus, who protected the doorway. (We still call a door-keeper the janitor, and the month January opens the year.) The Penates were special spirits who guarded the family's food stores. In wealthy families at mealtimes, the head of the household would put wine on the altar and throw a piece of salt-cake on the fire to please the spirits.

The Gods

Hundreds of gods and goddesses were worshipped by the Romans. The main ones were Jupiter, the father of the gods and god of rain, thunder and lightning, his wife, Juno, and Minerva, the goddess of healing and wisdom. Others

This is a highly decorated shrine, typical of those found in Roman houses, showing pictures of the household spirits.

Carving from a Mithraic temple.

Altar from the Temple of Vespasian.

included Mars (war), Neptune (the sea), Venus (love) and Mercury (messenger of the gods). All the important gods had their own temples and shrines. On special days the Romans would offer gifts of flowers or fruit to the gods. Sometimes they sacrificed animals as a gift or because they believed that they could tell the future from their entrails.

As the Romans expanded their Empire and traded around the ancient world, they came across many other gods worshipped by other peoples. They usually allowed people they had conquered to worship in their own way. The Roman army and the citizens of Rome sometimes adopted other people's gods as their own – the Persian god Mithras and the Egyptian goddess Isis were examples of this.

Mithras

Worship of Mithras became especially popular. Mithras was supposed to be a messenger between humans and the gods who had saved the Earth from evil forces. He had killed a sacred bull, whose blood was said to give life to plants and animals. Only men were allowed to worship Mithras. They did this in mysterious ceremonies, wearing coloured cloaks and masks. Followers of Mithras had to pass tests. For example, they would be blindfolded, shut in a coffin and made to endure extreme heat or bitter cold. Many Roman soldiers worshipped Mithras.

Emperor worship

From the reign of the Emperor Augustus (27 BC to AD 14), the Romans began to see their Emperors as gods. All over the Empire, Roman citizens were encouraged to build temples to the Emperor, and it was their duty to bring gifts to his sacred altar. The Roman army always celebrated the birthday of Augustus, on 23 September.

Christianity

The Christian faith also began to spread through the Roman Empire. Christians believed in one all-powerful God, and refused to agree to Emperor worship. They also objected to the cruel Roman sports held in the amphitheatres. Because the Christians followed a humble carpenter's son, not a powerful and wealthy ruler, this religion appealed to poor men and women. At first, they were persecuted (criticised, arrested, even killed) by the Roman authorities. They often had to worship in secret places like the underground caves of Rome, but their numbers grew. The ill-treatment ended in the fourth century AD, when the Emperor Constantine became a Christian. Christianity became the official religion of the Roman Empire under Emperor Theodosius in AD 392.

Questions

Section A

1 What were household spirits?

2 Study Source A. Do you think the Romans believed that the worship of household spirits was very important? Give reasons for your answer.

3 Name some of the main Roman gods and goddesses and what they were connected with, e.g. Mars – god of war.

4 Describe the worship of Mithras.

5 What do you think is happening in Source B? Explain your answer.

6 a Describe the scene in Source C.
b How many priests do you think there are in Source C? Give reasons for your answer.

Section B

7 If a Roman farmer's crops failed mysteriously one year, and his family went short of food, what might he think had caused his problems, and what might he do about it?

8 Four of the five temples to Mithras that have been found in Roman Britain are near the sites of Roman army settlements. Mithras was a popular god among soldiers.

a Why did Roman soldiers have a special need for religion?
b Why did Mithras appeal so much to soldiers?

9 Imagine that you are a spy sent among the Christians who are worshipping secretly in Rome to find out about their beliefs. Write a letter to the Emperor explaining why you think they must be persecuted.

Claudius Conquers Britain

The Emperor Claudius began his invasion of Britain in AD 43. This was nearly one hundred years after Julius Caesar's landings. As with Caesar, there were a number of possible reasons why Claudius wanted his troops to cross the Channel.

He may have needed a military victory to win the loyalty of the public and the army. The merchants and generals in Rome, who had most to gain from the conquest of Britain, may have talked him into it. Britain could produce wheat, metals and taxes for Rome. The Druids – a group of religious leaders among the Britons and the Gauls – had been causing trouble in Gaul, and Claudius may have wanted to strike at their base, which was in Britain.

The Rhine frontier was peaceful, so there were troops available in Germany. The Britons were divided; in AD 42 war broke out between rival British tribes, and one of them asked Rome for help. The time seemed right to invade.

The invasion almost failed before it set off. When the Roman ships gathered in Boulogne, the troops refused to get

Some of the key places involved in the conquest of Britain.

on board. Rumours had spread that Britain was full of demons and that the fleet could fall off the edge of the world – the Romans called Britain 'the islands at the end of the Earth'. Mutiny was near. But when a silly-looking lieutenant called Narcissus stood up to shout at them, the men fell about laughing, the tension broke and the troops poured on board.

Aulus Plautius was the general in charge of the invasion. His force of more than 40,000 men landed in the sheltered harbour of Richborough before moving inland. The leader of the Catuvellauni, **Caractacus**, was the legions' main opponent. The Romans won a hard two-day battle at the river Medway, then a shorter fight near the Thames, before they reached the new base of the Catuvellauni at Colchester. There the Roman army paused.

The Emperor Claudius arrived with important Roman public figures and a troop of elephants to add to the importance of the occasion and then the legions quickly overran British resistance. Claudius stayed in Colchester only sixteen days – long enough to accept the surrender of some of the British kings. He made Plautius governor of his new province, and returned in glory to Rome. The Emperor's two-year-old son was given a new name: Britannicus.

The conquest of Britain followed in four more waves. Between AD 43 and 47 the Romans advanced forward to a line running across the country from about Exeter to the Humber. Their most famous victory was by troops led by Vespasian at Maiden Castle in Dorset. They built the Fosse Way to help defend this frontier.

Between AD 48 and 51 the Roman Second Legion went after Caractacus, who had fled to join allies in the West. The legion defeated the British tribes in Gloucestershire, North Wales and then Yorkshire before they captured Caractacus.

Another stage in the conquest came between AD 59 and 61, when Suetonius Paulinus marched into North Wales and massacred the Druids in Anglesey. But this advance came to an end because of the dangerous rebellion in the South-East led by Queen Boudicca (see the next unit).

Roman control grew between AD 71 and 84, mainly under the new governor of Britain, Agricola. Agricola reconquered North Wales, northern England and southern Scotland.

The Romans never advanced further into the Highlands. Instead they decided to defend their northern border first with **Hadrian's Wall**, started in AD 122, and then with the **Antonine Wall**, begun in about AD 142. Roman control of Britain south of Hadrian's Wall stayed firm until about AD 360, when invaders from the Continent began to attack the coasts in large numbers. By this time, Rome itself was also under attack, and troops were often called back to Italy to defend the Empire's capital city. The last Roman soldiers left Britain in about AD 410.

Questions

Section A

1 Draw a time-line of the conquest of Britain from AD 42 to AD 410. Mark on it the events of this unit.

2 Draw the map in your book. The map is divided into different sections. Add a key showing when each section fell under Roman control.

Section B

3 Historians call the reasons why an event happens the **causes** of that event. They call a person's reasons for acting in one way rather than another that person's **motives**.

   a Write a list of Claudius's possible motives in attacking Britain.

   b Write a list of the other possible reasons for the invasion.

   c Do you think Claudius's actions when he came to Britain help us to understand his motives? Explain your answer.

4 a Some reasons for invading Britain in AD 43 had existed for many years. These were 'long-term causes'. Name one.

   b Some reasons for invading had become important only a short time before. These were 'short-term causes'. Name one.

5 'The conquest of Britain depended on a chance event when a silly-looking lieutenant, by accident, made the men laugh.' Write about fifty words supporting this statement. Then write about fifty words arguing against it.

Boudicca's Revolt

In AD 59 Suetonius Paulinus, an experienced general, was appointed governor of Britain by the Emperor Nero. Paulinus wanted to increase Roman control beyond the Fosse Way. He planned an attack on Anglesey, a large island off the north coast of Wales. Anglesey was the base of the British priests called **Druids**, whose religion involved human sacrifices in sacred oak groves. The Druids also acted as judges and advisers to many of the British tribes. Several kings looked to them for guidance, and many Britons who had fled from the Romans had gathered on Anglesey. Paulinus attacked Anglesey from North Wales in AD 60. The Druids were massacred without mercy and the sacred oak groves where they held their ceremonies were cut down.

Whilst he was in Anglesey, Paulinus heard that the Iceni had rebelled. The Iceni were a tribe who lived in present-day Norfolk. They had surrendered to the Romans in about AD 47, but many of them had suffered from Roman money-lenders and tax collectors. The Iceni were also followers of the Druids and made human sacrifices; they were angered by the killing of the Druids.

Earlier in AD 60, the king of the Iceni had died. He had no sons, so he had arranged for his wife, Boudicca, to become queen and for his wealth to be divided between his two daughters and the Emperor Nero. The Romans, though, wanted all of his wealth and power. Boudicca was flogged and her daughters were raped whilst Roman officials looted their palace and stole their lands.

The Iceni rebelled, killing every Roman they could find. Other tribes, each with its own reasons, joined the revolt. The Catuvellauni hated having to give up their land to retired Roman soldiers. The Trinovantes disliked the large temple at Colchester dedicated to Claudius which they had to pay for and where they were told to worship the Emperor as a god.

The rebels were successful. Colchester was overrun, and its inhabitants, Roman or otherwise – men, women and children – were slaughtered, many of them as they took refuge in the temple. Next, London was attacked and burned to the ground. Verulamium (St Albans) soon suffered the same fate. Possibly as many as 70,000 people lost their lives.

The Emperor Nero considered withdrawing all his troops from Britain, but before Nero could make up his mind, Paulinus acted. His army marched quickly back from Wales along the new Roman road, Watling Street, and he prepared for battle. Paulinus's 10,000 soldiers were outnumbered ten to one. But Boudicca's rebels had destroyed most of the Romans' food stores, and winter was approaching. They had to stand and fight or leave Britain.

Questions

1 The frames of the cartoon can be rearranged to tell the story of Boudicca. Copy them into your book in the right order. Give each frame a caption so that it explains the story of Boudicca's revolt.

2 From the description you have read of the fighting, draw a diagram to show what you think happened in the battle. Use a key and make sure your diagram includes: the trees, the wagons, the armies, the attacks, the retreat of the Britons.

Section B

3 The Romans normally allowed the people they conquered to follow their own religions. Why did Paulinus attack and kill the Druids? Write down the reasons under these headings:

 a Paulinus's personal motives (personal reasons).
 b How the Druids threatened Roman rule (strategic reasons).
 c Objections to the Druids' religion (religious reasons).

4 How did the Romans succeed against the British rebels? Write down the reasons under these headings:

 a The leadership of Paulinus.
 b The organisation of the Roman army.
 c The mistakes of the Britons.

5 'The Roman army was much better armed and better organised than the British. So the Romans were *bound to* defeat the rebellion in the end.' Do you agree? Give reasons for your answer.

Paulinus chose his ground well. He drew up his men on top of a slope, shielded by thick forest behind and woods on either side. The Britons were so sure of victory that they had brought their wives and children in carts behind them to watch the battle. They rushed their chariots in a disorganised charge up the slope into the narrow clearing. The Romans threw volleys of spears into their ranks and then advanced in a wedge formation, driving the Britons back. Roman auxiliaries on horseback skirted round the side of the fighting and killed the oxen pulling the carts at the rear. The retreat of the Britons came to a halt as they stumbled through fallen horses, chariots, bodies and then the carts, which were now impossible to move.

All of the Britons and their families were killed mercilessly. The revolt was at an end. Boudicca escaped from the battle but is said to have taken poison to avoid capture.

Religion in Roman Britain

The Britons, like the Romans and many pagan people before them, believed that spirits existed among the everyday things around them. How else could they explain mysteries like hailstorms, floods, the wind and the growth of crops? They worshipped the sun and the moon, as well as hundreds more gods and goddesses among the rivers, forests and mountains. Some gods were local, like the river gods Deva and Sabrina, which gave their names to the rivers Dee and Severn. Some were worshipped by whole tribes, like Brigantia, the goddess of the Brigantes in northern England. Other gods were linked with special activities, like Nodens, god of hunting.

Pigs, bulls, dogs and snakes were the Britons' sacred animals and were often sacrificed to the gods. Simple shrines, often of wood, served as temples, and small glades of trees were also used as open–air places of worship.

After the conquest and Emperor worship

When the Romans invaded Britain, they found many of the British gods similar to their own. They mostly allowed the Britons to continue to worship their gods. Some Romans even believed that British gods were Roman gods in disguise; there are many examples of temples for the worship of British and Roman gods together. The British god Sulis of the hot springs at Bath was combined with the Roman goddess Minerva, and the Romans built a magnificent temple to Sulis-Minerva next to the baths there.

But there were problems. The Romans wanted the Britons to worship their Emperors. A huge temple was built at Colchester to the Emperor Claudius. The Britons were expected to pay for the statue of the Emperor that was in the centre of the temple. It is likely that many Britons were angry at this, and it was probably one cause of the revolt by the Iceni under Boudicca in AD 60. Emperor worship was never popular in Britain.

Druids and Christians

The Romans would not tolerate the Druids. The last chapter showed how Druidism was wiped out by Paulinus in AD 60. The Druids were the powerful high priests of the British tribes. They held mysterious religious services in groves of oak trees, where they would climb an oak and cut mistletoe

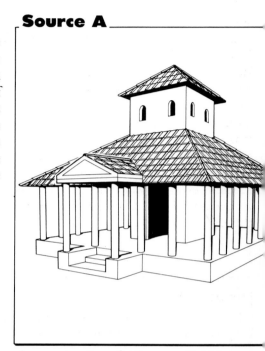

A reconstruction of a Romano-British temple at Silchester.

The Chi-Rho monogram, a symbol of the Christian Church, on the wall of a hidden private chapel in a Roman villa at Lullingstone.

with a golden knife before using the same blade to sacrifice an animal, a prisoner or even a child. The Druids would predict the future from the twitchings of the body. Besides being the religious leaders of the Celts, they acted as judges and as political advisers to the tribal chiefs.

Christianity entered Britain during the Roman occupation. We know little about the earliest Christians. They preached that there was just one God and refused to worship the Emperors. Because of this they were persecuted by the Romans for many years and had to worship in secret. One Briton who had served seven years with the legions was executed by the Roman soldiers, probably in AD 209, for hiding a Christian priest. His name was **Albanus**. A shrine was built in his memory, then a monastery, and later the town of St Albans grew up there. Christianity gradually became accepted throughout the Roman Empire. In AD 313 the Emperor Constantine announced that all religions would be permitted; and Christianity became the official religion of the Empire in AD 392.

Source C

A wall painting from the villa at Lullingstone.

Questions

Section A

1 The beginnings and endings of the following sentences have been mixed up. Match the correct heads and tails:

Heads	Tails
a Before the Romans came, the Britons	usually allowed conquered people to keep their own gods.
b The Romans	worshipped the sun and moon as well as spirits of the woods and rivers.
c One religion which the Romans tried to impose upon the Britons was	the Druids.
d The Romans never tolerated the British religious group known as	Christianity.
e A religion which slowly became widespread in Britain after the Romans came was	Emperor worship.

2 a Describe what is happening in Source C.
   b Which religion do these people belong to? Give reasons for your answer.

Section B

3 Imagine that you are the Roman Emperor Claudius just after the Roman conquest. You want to govern the new province well. Explain the advantages and disadvantages, from your point of view, of:

   a allowing the Britons to keep their own gods and goddesses;
   b encouraging the Britons to adopt Emperor worship;
   c killing the Druids.

   (All these policies were used by the Romans at one time or another).

4 The Britons used 'simple shrines, often of wood' or open-air glades of trees. The Romans built temples like Source A. Does this mean that the Britons were less religious?

5 The Druids practised human sacrifice. Do you think that this means they enjoyed killing people?

Roman Roads in Britain

Source A

The remains of a Roman road. You should be able to see the foundation layer and the drainage ditch.

Source B

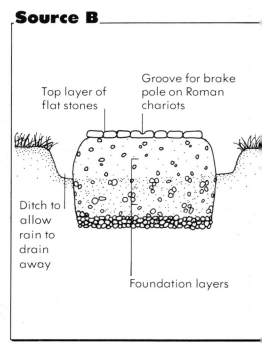

Top layer of flat stones

Groove for brake pole on Roman chariots

Ditch to allow rain to drain away

Foundation layers

A cross-section of a Roman road.

By AD 47, within four years of their invasion, the Romans had built almost 1,000 miles of roads. These roads were mainly for the army. The Roman legions needed to be able to march quickly to areas of trouble, as they did to put down Boudicca's revolt. Army generals had to gather news and send orders speedily, and the roads helped provide reliable supplies of food and reinforcements. Once an area was peaceful, the Romans still needed roads for government and tax collecting. Then traders would begin to use the roads to get grain, animals, metals and other goods to the army camps and the towns.

Once Roman rule was strong, thousands of Roman soldiers, officials, merchants and their families settled in Britain. Roman soldiers married British women, and Britons joined the Roman army. Britain's first true towns and cities began to grow, usually where there was an army camp. The towns had a Roman **forum** (market square), **basilica** (council building), baths, theatres, temple and town houses. Town life was impossible without good roads for trade, travel and food supplies.

The Romans built altogether more than 6,000 miles of roadways. You can study these roads from many different sources.

Source C

Building the roads

'The Roman engineer would sight the direction with the aid of an instrument called the "groma". It had a number of strings, each with a small weight on the end. The strings were lined up with a pole a hundred metres or so away. A survey party was sent forward to light a fire at the best point and then pile on leaves and grass so that the smoke could be seen over great distances. As soon as the correct alignment had been decided, the digging was started. Two parallel ditches were made, one on each side of the line. The earth was piled in the space in between and rammed down. Layers of harder material were then added one at a time.'

From R.E.C. Burrell, 'The Romans in Britain' (Pergamon Press, 1972).

Source D

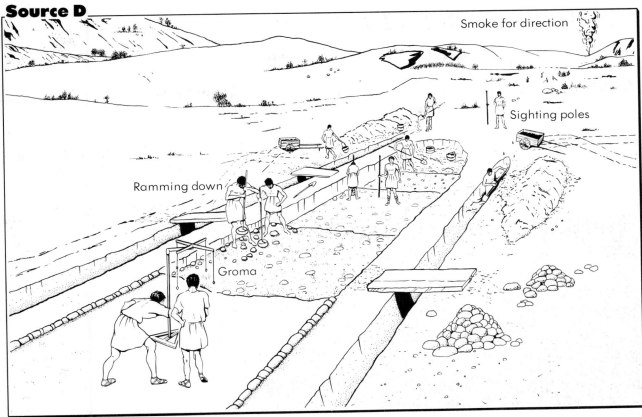

Smoke for direction

Sighting poles

Ramming down

Groma

An artist's reconstruction of Roman roadbuilding.

Questions

Section A

1 Explain at least five ways in which roads were important to the Romans in Britain.

2 Draw a cross-section of a Roman road.

3 How do Sources A and B help you to show that the Romans thought roads were very important?

Section B

4 Is Source A a primary or a secondary source? Give reasons for your answer.

5 Is Source B a primary or a secondary source? Give reasons for your answer.

6 Do Sources A and D agree at all about Roman roads? Explain your answer.

7 Do Sources B and D agree at all about Roman roads? Explain your answer.

8 Do Sources C and D agree at all about Roman roads? Explain your answer.

9 Source D is a secondary source (that means it is based on information from other sources). Which of these statements about secondary sources do you think is the best?

  a Secondary sources are based on primary sources.
  b Secondary sources are based on both primary sources and other secondary sources.
  c Secondary sources are based just on other secondary sources.
Explain your answer.

Hadrian's Wall

Hadrian's Wall.

I n AD 117 a revolt by tribes in Scotland and northern England led to heavy Roman losses. The Emperor Hadrian visited the northern part of his province in AD 121. He decided that because Caledonia (the Roman name for Scotland) would be expensive and difficult to conquer, he would build a wall to 'separate the Romans from the barbarians'. The wall was to stretch 117 km across Britain, from Bowness-on-Solway in the west to Wallsend-on-Tyne in the east. (See the map on page 36.)

Hadrian's Wall was built of stone, and had a ditch on either side. About 2 million cubic metres of earth had to be moved to dig the ditches and build it. Roman soldiers were trained in construction, and local labour from British tribes was also used. The job took many years to complete. First the foundations were laid, then two outer walls of stone were built, and the centre was packed with earth and rubble. This made a wall five or six metres high, with a walkway about two metres wide.

More than 10,000 soldiers guarded Hadrian's Wall against attack from the north. These troops were mainly stationed in **cohorts** (500 men) in sixteen forts, spread along the wall at 8 km intervals. One of the best known forts, which can still be seen, is at Housesteads. Between the forts would be **milecastles** spaced one Roman mile (about 1,500 metres) apart. Each milecastle housed between 30 and 100 soldiers. In between these were small sentry turrets manned by two soldiers who acted as look-outs. They could send smoke-signals to warn of attacks. To the north of the wall a defensive V-shaped ditch was dug, and some distance behind the wall was a smaller flat-bottomed ditch called the **vallum**.

An aerial photograph of Housesteads, a fort on Hadrian's Wall.

The latrines at Housesteads.

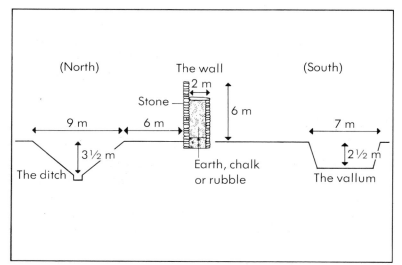

(North)   The wall   (South)

2 m

Stone

9 m   6 m   6 m   7 m

3½ m   2½ m

The ditch   Earth, chalk or rubble   The vallum

A diagram of the defences.

The only roads which crossed the wall passed over the vallum and through gates in the walls at the forts and milecastles. So the wall acted like a modern customs post as well as being a defensive barrier.

Questions

Section A

1 Explain why Hadrian's Wall was built.

2 Write a description of Hadrian's Wall, using these headings:

   a Where the wall was built.
   b How the wall was built.
   c Defensive features.

3 Draw a plan of a 10 km stretch of the wall and show on it forts, milecastles and turrets.

Section B

4 Look at Source C. Various parts of the building remain. Using this source only, can you work out how the building was used?

5 Using the sources as evidence, say whether you think the following statements are true or false. Explain your answers.

   a The Romans were good builders.
   b Only British troops were used to garrison Hadrian's Wall.
   c The Romans had a strong, well-run government.

6 Read your answer to question 4 and compare it to Source E.

   a Which is the better explanation of the toilets?
   b Which parts of Source E do you think could not be worked out using the archaeological evidence?
   c The historian who wrote Source E is used to interpreting sources. Is this the only advantage he had over you in working out how the toilets were used?

Source D

This altar stone was found in the fort of Carrawburgh, one of the forts built into Hadrian's Wall. The inscription on the stone reads: 'Sacred to Mithras, Aulus Cluentius Habitus, prefect of the First Cohort of Batavian from Larinium, willingly fulfilled his vow.' Only Roman officers were allowed to worship Mithras. Larinium was a place in Italy.

Source E

'There was no privacy. Soldiers sat side by side on wooden seats over the deep sewers running either side of the building. Toilet paper had not been invented. Soldiers cleaned themselves with a sponge on the end of a stick which they dipped into the narrow channels of water at their feet. They would then wash their hands in one of the two stone washbasins in the centre of the room.'

From Warren Farnworth, 'Roman Britain' (Bell & Hyman, 1979).

The End of Roman Britain

Claudius's invasion had begun in AD 43. By AD 47 the Romans had reached the Fosse Way, and they advanced further across Britain between AD 71 and 84. Hadrian's Wall was started in AD 122, and north of that, the Antonine Wall was built about the year AD 142. The attacks of the tribes in Scotland forced the Romans to retreat from this second wall by about AD 180. But they completely controlled the land south of Hadrian's Wall.

Roman rule had brought peace to southern Britain, but Rome itself was becoming weaker. Warlike tribes from central Europe attacked the Roman Empire's borders. Sometimes they swarmed across the frontiers. The Romans became more and more worried. Troops were brought back from Britain to help fight the **barbarians**.

Fewer Roman soldiers were left to protect Britain, and attacks on the provinces increased. The Picts raided from the north of Hadrian's Wall. Saxon sea-pirates from across the North Sea began to attack the east and south coasts from the late third century onwards.

From about AD 270 the Romans began to build forts from Norfolk to Hampshire to protect the coastline closest to Europe. The Romans called these the **Forts of the Saxon Shore,** and their commander was known as the Count of the Saxon Shore. By AD 350 there were at least ten of these forts. Each was rectangular in shape with 30 foot high walls and round towers to shoot catapults from.

The forts acted as bases for the **Classis Britannica,** the Roman fleet in Britain. This consisted of fast, light scout-ships, camouflaged in sea green or blue, and powered by twenty oarsmen. The forts and fleet were meant to guard harbours and river-mouths from attack and to drive away invaders.

In AD 286 Carausius, the commander of the Classis Britannica, rebelled against the Emperor Diocletian and set himself up as 'the Emperor in Britain'. He took soldiers from all over Britain to help fight off an attack by the Roman Emperor's armies, and this civil war lasted ten years.

By this time, the Picts had overrun the weakened Hadrian's Wall, and it took some years to drive them back. But the attacks continued. In AD 343 things were so bad that the Emperor Constans crossed the Channel in winter to visit the wall personally.

The worst attack came in AD 367. The Picts, Saxons and Scots launched attacks at the same time, and the weakened

Source A

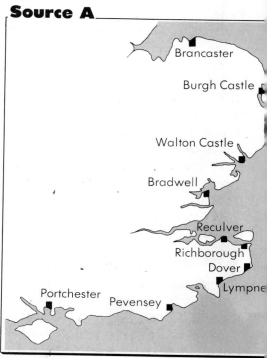

Forts of the Saxon shore.

Source B

An aerial photograph of Richborough Castle. This site was used by the Romans at different times as a stone-walled fort, a monument to celebrate the conquest of Britain by Claudius and a fort protected by banks and ditches.

Roman legions couldn't resist them. The Count of the Saxon Shore was killed in battle, the Scots raided as far south as Kent, and London was besieged. For almost a year people lived in fear as invaders destroyed villas, towns and villages. In the end the Emperor Theodosius restored order, but life never returned to normal.

In AD 383 the Emperor Maximus took more troops from Britain. The Picts again saw this as an opportunity to attack Hadrian's Wall. They completely overran it, and the wall was never refortified. The boundaries of Roman Britain were shrinking.

By this time the Saxons weren't just raiding Britain. In some places the British chiefs realised that the Romans could no longer protect them. They invited Saxon leaders into Britain to settle, if they promised to help drive off other invaders.

In AD 401 the Emperor Honorius took still more troops away to defend Rome, and in AD 407 the military commander took away perhaps the last Roman soldiers in Britain to fight in Gaul. In AD 410, when the Britons pleaded with the Emperor for help against the Saxons, they were told they would have to defend themselves. Even the city of Rome was now surrounded by enemies, and Roman Britain was at an end.

Questions

Section A

1 a Copy Source A into your book.
   b Look at a map of Europe in an atlas, and see where the sites of the Forts of the Saxon Shore are. Where do you think the invaders the Romans were worried about were coming from?
   c Does Source A **prove** that the greatest threat to Roman Britain was from these sea-faring invaders?

2 a Trace or sketch the main features of the site shown in Source B. Pick out and label the parts which you think remain from each of the three uses of the site.
   b What order do you think the three uses of Richborough came in? Give reasons for your answer and, if you can, suggest dates for each use.

Section B

3 Draw a time-line from AD 43 to AD 600. Mark on it all the events mentioned in this unit. (You'll need plenty of space!)

4 When you have marked on your time-line the *events* and the *years* when they happened, think about the *stages* or *periods* of the Roman occupation. Draw another time-line and divide it into three stages:

   a Roman conquest of Britain.
   b The Romans in control of Britain.
   c The decline of Roman Britain.

   Compare your stages with other people's. You might not agree exactly. Historical periods sometimes don't have exact beginnings and endings.

5 If Roman Britain starts in AD 43, when does it end: AD 343?, AD 367?, AD 383?, AD 410? Make your choice and explain your reasons.

6 Do you think there is only one right answer to question 5? Give reasons for your answer.

Who Were the Saxons? The Written Sources

After the Roman armies had gone, the Britons were attacked by seafaring Angles, Saxons and Jutes. These were warlike German tribes whose homelands were colder and less fertile than Britain. Picts and other tribes from the North and Scotland also made raids on southern Britain. Like the Romans had before them, the Britons tried to pay some of these 'barbarian' warriors to keep the others away.

In about AD 450 Vortigern, a British king, asked the Jute warrior leaders Hengest and Horsa to help him fight off the Picts; he gave the Jutes the Isle of Thanet in Kent as reward. These warriors then turned against Vortigern, and Hengest made himself king of Kent. The news spread that Britain was badly defended, and the numbers of raiders crossing the sea increased. The newcomers began to make their homes in Britain, attracted by the fertile soil and warmer climate. The Celtic Britons were driven back westwards, into Wales, Cornwall and the North West.

We know very little about these invaders. The two centuries after the Romans left are called the **Dark Ages**, partly because of the lack of information about these times, and partly because the 'light' of Roman civilisation had gone. The invaders were illiterate and left no written records describing themselves. We have to rely upon the writings of their enemies the Britons, or those of later Anglo-Saxon writers.

For example, there was Gildas, a British monk. About the year AD 540 Gildas wrote *The Ruin of Britain*, telling the story of Britons slaughtered and driven from their homes. He regarded the barbarian invasions as a punishment sent by God, because of the sins of the people. Gildas's writings were intended to be a warning to the Britons as much as a historical record.

Another written source is by the Venerable Bede, a monk who grew up in Northumbria. In AD 731 Bede finished his *History of the English Church and People*. He wrote as an historian, to record information, and as a teacher, to educate. His style is clear, less emotional than that of Gildas, but he sometimes oversimplified events.

A third source is *The Anglo-Saxon Chronicle*. This book was written as a year-by-year account of events in the Anglo-Saxon kingdoms by many different monks over many years. It was not started until about four hundred years after the invasions, so the sections on the early years are sketchy and sometimes inaccurate.

Source A

'They landed on the eastern side of the island by invitation of the unfortunate king, and fixed their sharp talons, apparently to fight in favour of the island, but alas more truly against it. From that time their germ planted poison amongst us, as we deserved.'

Activities

a Source A describes the invaders as violent and cruel people. List three words which give this impression.

b The source seems to sympathise with the Britons. Which phrase gives this impression?

c Do you think the source comes from Gildas, Bede or *The Anglo-Saxon Chronicle*? Explain your choice.

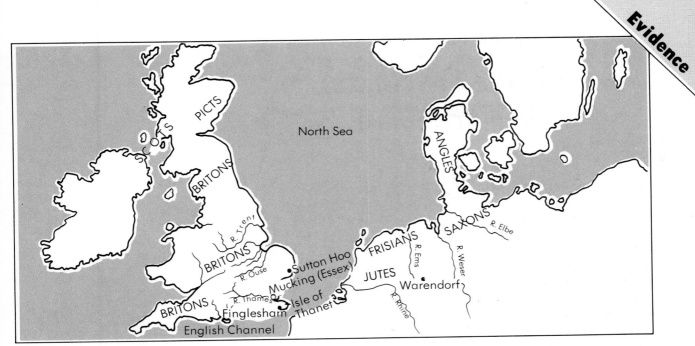

The Anglo-Saxon invasions.

Source B

'They laid down their beloved lord, their
    treasure giver,
In splendour by the mast, in the bosom of
    the ship.
A mass of treasure was brought there from
    distant parts.
No ship, they say was ever so well
    equipped with swords, weapons and
    armour.'

'Then warriors rode round the barrow.
They praised his manhood and the
    prowess of his hands,
They raised his name; it is right a man
Should be lavish in honouring his lord.'

Descriptions of the funerals of Anglo-Saxon kings, from 'Beowulf'.

Activity

Divide into groups of four. In each group, one person must describe to the others any recent event in his or her life. Next, each of the others in the group must retell the story — one making it as sad, one as exciting and the other as romantic as possible. Write down a list of all the ways in which the stories were changed as they were retold.

Poems about warrior heroes, passed on by word of mouth and later written down, are also important written sources. The best known is *Beowulf* (see source B), the story of a legendary warrior, written about AD 750.

Questions

Section A

1 a Write a list of the names of the invading tribes.
  b Where did each tribe come from?

2 Write out the following passage and fill in the spaces, using the list of words provided.

The ..... were the people who lived in Britain before the Romans came and who were left behind when the Romans left. From about AD 400 they were forced westwards by the invaders into ..... and ..... . The ..... were the people who invaded Britain in growing numbers from about AD 400. They came from ..... . Once they had settled in large parts of the country, they became known as the ..... .

Northern Europe   English   Anglo-Saxons
Wales   Britons   Cornwall

Section B

3 'The people in the poem *Beowulf* never really lived. It is a made-up story.' Does this mean that historians will not find it a useful source?

4 a We have evidence of the Anglo-Saxon invaders in the writings of Gildas, Bede, *The Anglo-Saxon Chronicle* and the poems. Which would you trust the most? Explain why.
  b Can any of these written sources give us a complete or completely fair picture of the Anglo-Saxons?

Who Were the Saxons? Other Evidence

Written records of the invading tribes are few and difficult to use. So historians have to rely upon other types of evidence to build up a clearer picture of the people who began to settle in Britain during the fifth century.

Archaeologists have found remains of Saxon settlements on the Continent and in Britain which tell us about their lives. One such site is at Warendorf, in Germany. This gives evidence of houses more than 24 metres long, with a number of smaller outhouses and stables. These buildings were wooden, with thatched roofs, and researchers can work out their shape from post-holes in the ground.

Source B

Sword found in a grave at Finglesham.

Source A

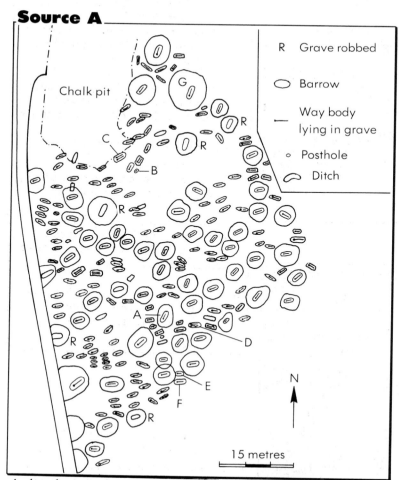

R	Grave robbed
⬭	Barrow
⊢	Way body lying in grave
∘	Posthole
⌒	Ditch

Chalk pit

N

15 metres

Archaeologist's plan of a Saxon cemetery at Finglesham, Kent, based on an excavation.

Source C

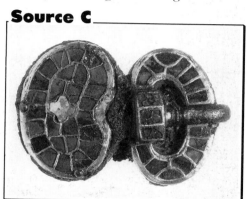

Silver jewelled buckle found in a grave at Finglesham.

Anglo-Saxon **burial customs** are another useful source of information. The northern tribes had a strong belief in the afterlife. Corpses were buried with all the belongings people were thought to need after death. When these graves are opened up, the personal possessions inside tell us much about how the Anglo-Saxons lived.

An Anglo-Saxon cemetery has been excavated at Finglesham in Kent. It contains almost 250 graves, dating from about AD 525. Some women were buried in fine clothes held together with ornamental pins and silver brooches. They had beads around their necks and combs to improve their appearance in the next world. Men were often buried with their shields, spears, helmets and swords. The richest graves at Finglesham were found under **barrows** – large burial mounds provided for rich and powerful people. Other graves with simpler possessions inside were scattered between the mounds. The skeletons include many children and young people. There is little evidence about how people died, though one man's skull had been split.

Source D

The Saxon settlement at Warendorf.

Source E

Questions

Section A

1 Using Sources A – E as evidence, say whether the following statements are true or false. Give reasons for your answers.

   a The Saxons were great builders in stone.
   b The Saxons were skilled metalworkers.
   c The Saxons believed in life after death.

Section B

2 Is Source D a primary or a secondary source? Explain your answer.

3 Is Source E a primary or a secondary source? Explain your answer.

4 Compare Sources D and E.

   a What important information about buildings **can** historians find out from post-holes?
   b What important information about buildings can historians **not** find out from post-holes?

5 Study Source A. Which of the graves a – g were for children and which were for adults? Explain your answer.

6 Grave d has two bodies in it.

   a Is this common?
   b What reasons can you think of why this might have happened?

7 Sources B and C were both found in one grave. Which of the graves e, f or g do you think they came from? Give reasons for your answer.

8 Do you think the person buried with Sources B and C was male or female? Give reasons for your answer.

Archaeologist's excavation of a Saxon hall at Mucking, Essex, showing post-holes. The building was about 6.5 metres by 13 metres. Only one end is seen here. What do you think post-holes are?

51

Who Were the Saxons? Ships

We know that the Anglo-Saxon invaders must have come to Britain in ships, and we also know quite a lot about the ships they came in. We know this because the remains of some of the ships have been found by archaeologists both in mainland Europe and in Britain.

The **Nydam ship** was discovered about a hundred years ago at Nydam, near Germany's border with Denmark, preserved in a peat bog. This must have been the type of craft used by the invaders. It is about 23.5 metres long and 3 metres wide, with sides low enough for the fourteen oars to be used over the gunwales, and a keel too weak to carry a mast and sail. In the open seas, such ships were extremely unsafe, and a crossing of the North Sea was treacherous. The invaders must have been brave and eager to risk the journey to Britain.

One of the most famous and most puzzling ships to be found was discovered in a field at **Sutton Hoo** in Suffolk in 1939. Sutton Hoo is about 10 km from the coast, overlooking the estuary of the river Deben. There are about fifteen large mounds at the site, one of which was excavated by archaeologists in 1939. They found the remains of a boat about 24 metres long. They carefully exposed the dark layers of sand left by the rotting wooden planks of the boat's hull, so that its overall shape could be seen.

The problem is, why was this boat where it was? We might expect boats to be found in or near the sea, but not 10 km inland.

Source B

The framework of the Sutton Hoo ship revealed during excavations.

Source A

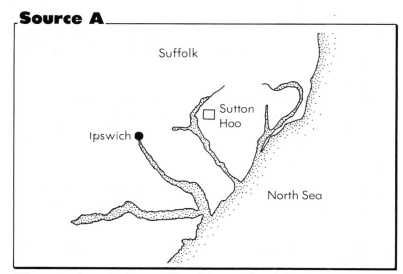

The area where the Sutton Hoo ship was found.

Possible solution one

The ship was wrecked and sank or was abandoned.
   Use Sources A and B either to support or to reject this solution.

Source C

'Archaeologists found a collection of objects on the ship: a sceptre, a lyre, a helmet, a sword, other weapons, armour, drinking dishes, jewellery, spoons, bowls, a bronze cauldron and a hoard of coins from all over Europe.'

Source D

A ship found buried under a mound at Oseberg in Norway. The ship contained the bodies of two women and many of their belongings.

Possible solution two

The site at Sutton Hoo was the Saxon equivalent of a shipyard, and the Sutton Hoo ship was being built.

Use Sources A, B and C either to support or to reject this solution.

Possible solution three

This time you must come up with your own solution. It should be the most likely explanation you can think of for why the ship was found in the field.

Historians always try to get their ideas from as wide a range of sources as possible. You might find it a good idea to use some of the information about the Saxons on pages 48–51 – try *Beowulf* on page 49 and the cemetery at Finglesham on pages 50–51.

Questions

Who were the Saxons? Conclusions

To answer the following questions, you should use all of the information about the Saxons in the last three units.

Section A

1 Sketch or trace the outline map in Saxons 3.1, then plot a possible route for Saxon invaders from Warendorf to Sutton Hoo. Be careful: the best answer is not necessarily the most obvious route.

2 Copy out the following sentences, choosing the best alternative words. See if you can support each statement with both written and non-written sources:

  a The Saxons were warlike/peaceful people.
  b The Saxons were artistic people/not interested in art.
  c The Saxons were/were not religious people.
  d The Saxons lived in communities/small family groups.
  e The Saxons were all poor/all rich/a mixture of rich and poor.

Section B

3 What has the non-written evidence of the last two units been able to tell historians which they couldn't get from the written sources?

4 Describe one advantage and one disadvantage of non-written evidence.

53

King Arthur: Legend or History?

Two hundred years after the first Anglo-Saxon invasions, the Celtic Britons had been driven deep into the western corners of the country – Wales, Cornwall and the Lake District. The Britons won very few battles. But their victory at the battle of Badon Hill, in the West Country, in the year AD 518, seems to have stopped the Saxon advance for roughly fifty years.

Stories have existed for many centuries of a heroic leader among the Britons who rallied his people and for a time held back the Saxon flood. The minstrels and story-tellers of the Middle Ages described him as a great warrior king. They named him Arthur (which means 'the bear'), but we know little about this mysterious and romantic figure.

Who was Arthur? Was he the heroic warrior the stories claim? Did he really exist at all?

Source A

'Some Britons were murdered; others yielded themselves to be slaves; some others passed beyond the seas. Some took up arms under Ambrosius. To these men there came victory and this continued up to the year of Badon Hill, the last great slaughter of the rascally crew of Saxons.'

From Gildas, 'The Ruin of Britain', c. AD 540. The British monk Gildas was born at about the time of the battle of Badon Hill. He wrote a bitter account of his times and was critical of his countrymen.

Source B

'The war leader Arthur's twelfth battle was on Mount Badon, in which there fell on one day nine hundred and sixty men from the onslaught of Arthur only, and no one killed them save he alone. In all of his battles he was the victor.'

From Nennius, 'A History of Britain', c. AD 800. Nennius was a Welsh monk who recorded a long list of Arthur's victories.

Source C

'Arthur told his men, "These foreign tongued people lack the courage of us Christians." Towards the evening Arthur fell upon Medrod's army and tore it apart as a lion scatters tame animals. He killed Medrod and thousands with him. And there also Arthur was wounded unto death and they carried him away from the battlefield.'

From Geoffrey of Monmouth, 'History of the Kings of England', c. AD 1136. Geoffrey of Monmouth lived in the twelfth century. His book, in which he named King Arthur as the brother of Ambrosius, was based upon legends and folk-tales.

Source D

'At south Cadbury standeth Camelot, sometime a famous town or castle. The people there can tell nothing, but that they have heard say that Arthur was often at Camelot.'

From John Leland, 'Itinerary', c. 1544. Leland travelled Britain and produced a survey of historic sites for King Henry VIII.

Source E

'Post-holes of a wooden building of some size have been found.
Fragments of fifth-century wine-pots from the Mediterranean area
have been found. Ordinary people could not have afforded
imported wine, so those who inhabited the site at this time must have
had the wealth and contacts to afford it. Similar fragments have
been found at Glastonbury Tor and Tintagel.'

From an archaeological survey of Cadbury Castle, 1967.

Archaeologist's drawing of Cadbury.

Source F

'Archaeologists have searched for the site of Camelot. However, a
number of places are linked with Arthur; for example, Tintagel and
Glastonbury in South West England, and there is an Arthur's
Stone in Glamorgan, Wales. Holy relics and the tombs of famous
people were the medieval equivalent of the modern tourist
attractions. Many poorer as well as wealthy people went on
pilgrimages to places like Glastonbury Abbey.'

*From J.A.P. Jones, 'History in the Making: 2 The Medieval
World' (Macmillan, 1979).*

Source G

'None of the scenes of Arthur's battles have been found.'

From John Hamer, 'King Arthur – Legend or History', 1983.

Source H

A nineteenth-century illustration of Camelot.

Questions

Section A

1 What picture of Arthur do you get from:

   Source A?, Source B?, Source C?

2 Why do you think the sources disagree about Arthur?

3 Which one of the three Sources (A – C) is likely to be the most reliable? Explain your answer.

Section B

4 a Look at Sources E and H. Which of these buildings would the one at South Cadbury have been most like?

   b Do you think King Arthur had a palace at South Cadbury?

   Explain your answers.

5 After reading all the sources, do you think King Arthur existed? You could debate this in class. Those who think he did exist should describe him in as much detail as possible, giving evidence for every detail. Those who do not think he existed must explain why they reject the evidence of his having lived and why his legend has lasted so long.

6 'If the story of Arthur is only legend, it is untrue and so it is useless to historians.' Do you agree?

Saxon Settlement

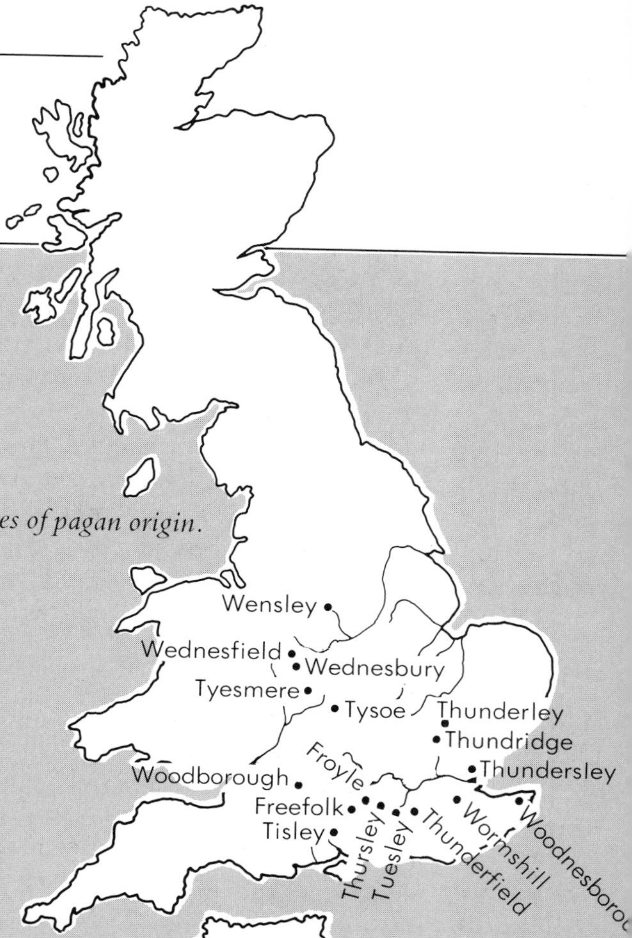

Some place names of pagan origin.

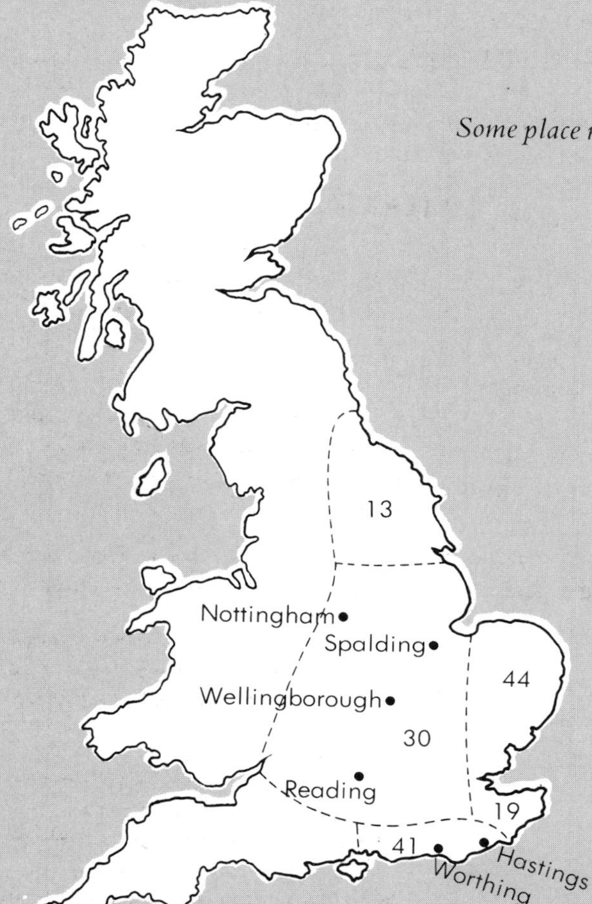

Wensley
Wednesfield • • Wednesbury
Tyesmere • • Tysoe Thunderley
• Thundridge
Woodborough • Froyle • Thundersley
Freefolk • • Wormshill • Woodnesborou
Tisley • • Thurderfield
Thursley Tuesley

13

Nottingham •
Spalding •
Wellingborough • 44
30
Reading •
19
41 • • Hastings
Worthing

Place names containing the letters 'ing'.
The numbers within the dotted lines show
how many place names containing 'ing'
have been found. Some examples are
given.

Anglo-Saxon burial sites.

The written evidence of Gildas, Bede and the *Chronicles* tells us when the invaders came to Britain. The archaeological evidence, like the grave contents, gives us clues about what the Anglo-Saxons were like. But it is harder to find out when, how and where the newcomers settled.

One clue comes from **place-names**. The first Saxon settlements were named after the groups who landed first. Thus Hastings was named after the *ingas* or people of a leader called Hasta. Lots of towns have *-ing* in their name, and this shows that the Anglo-Saxons settled there. Later place names include other Saxon words, such as *-burgh*, a fortified place, *-ton*, a village, and *-ham*, an isolated farmhouse. Other endings which show Saxon settlements are *-mouth*, *-water*, *-pool*, *-ly*, *-ley* or *-leigh*, *-worth* and *-stead*. The number of Saxon name-endings in any area gives us an idea of how much that area was settled by the Saxons. Look at the map which shows the location of English towns with *-ing* in their names.

There is a problem with using place-names as a guide. Just as the Saxon invaders changed the names of places where they settled, so the Vikings and the Normans may have changed the names again when they invaded later. This may have destroyed the true picture of Saxon settlement.

The Saxons sometimes dedicated their settlements to their gods and goddesses. They were heathens (non-Christians) and worshipped Tiw and Woden, the gods of war, Thunor 'the thunderer', Frig, the goddess of fertility, and many others. **Centres of worship** were named after these gods, and you can see the scatter of such places in the map which shows names of pagan origin.

Again, there are dangers in using this evidence. We cannot be sure that a pagan place-name means that the people who lived there were Saxons. The inhabitants may have been Britons who had adopted Saxon gods.

Saxon **cemeteries** are also useful sources. The location of these can show where the Saxons settled; dating the contents of graves can tell us when the Saxons arrived in that area; the number of graves shows how many Saxons were there. There seem to be a few early fifth-century sites and a large increase in the sixth century. The burial sites are most common in Kent and some other coastal areas and are mostly more scattered inland. Look at the map which shows the position of Saxon burial sites over the English countryside.

Once again, it is not certain that the cemeteries that have been unearthed give us a true picture of where the Saxons lived. The shallow graves of the Saxons may easily be destroyed by ploughing or quarrying, and can easily be built upon. Who knows how many other cemeteries lie undiscovered?

Questions

Section A

1 Explain why each of the following sources gives useful evidence about the spread of the Saxons in England:

   a Place-names.
   b Burial sites.

2 List some of the problems historians must remember when interpreting these sources.

3 Which modern English words do we use every week based on the names of the Saxon gods Tiw, Woden, Thunor and Frig?

Section B

4 Take an Ordnance Survey map of your area and see how many place-names with Saxon endings you can find. Do you think your area was overrun by the Saxons?

5 What name might the Saxons have given to a place marked by the farmhouse of the people of a leader called Beorma?

6 a Trace the map showing you where Saxon settlements with the ending *-ing* are.
   b Place your tracing over the map showing where the Saxon sites of pagan origin were. Put shading on your tracing to show where the pagan sites were.
   c Place your tracing on the map showing where the Saxon burial sites have been found. Put these burial sites on your tracing.
   d Can you now say *where* the Saxon invaders settled?

7 a Mark on your tracing the major rivers in England shown on the maps opposite.
   b Can you now tell *how* the invaders spread across England?

8 Can the place-names and burial sites help us tell *when* each area of England was settled by the Saxons?

Government and Society

As we have seen, the invasions of Angles, Saxons, Jutes and Frisians began about the year AD 400. Two hundred years later most of what we now call England was under their control. At first many separate small kingdoms were set up, but these gradually merged into seven large ones: Northumbria, Mercia, Essex, Middlesex, Kent, Sussex and Wessex.

The early Saxon kingdoms.

Northumbria was the most powerful kingdom in the seventh century, Mercia was strongest in the eighth century. In the tenth century the royal family of Wessex united the whole of Saxon England under one ruler. So in these years the English nation began to form. The old Roman ways were forgotten, and the Britons gave way to the Saxons. What kind of society did the Saxons bring to England?

Saxon kings were war leaders. They could demand service in the royal army, or **fyrd**, from their followers. They also had to keep order, give out justice and collect enough money to run the kingdom. Their personal qualities were so important that the sons of kings did not automatically inherit the throne. Each king chose as his successor the most suitable male of royal birth.

Kings ruled with the aid of the **thanes**. These were the nobles, who might be appointed as **eorls** to run parts of the kingdom, or might be members of the **Witan**, a council of 'wise men' which advised the king on important decisions. The early Saxon kingdoms had no capital where the ruler lived. He would have to travel around his lands to ensure good order. As he journeyed he would live on the food-taxes, or **feorms**, collected all over the kingdom by royal officials known as **reeves**.

At the heart of the Saxon kingdoms were the **ceorls**, or **churls**. These small farmers cultivated an area of about one **hide**, enough to support a family. They provided the kingdom with food, taxes and soldiers. Although their lives were hard, they were free men, and if their farms were successful enough they could themselves become thanes.

Lowest of all in Saxon society were the **thralls**, or slaves. These may have been the descendants of slaves, or captured Britons, or those who had fallen on hard times and had been forced to put themselves in the ownership of anyone who would clothe and feed them. Thralls were the property of their owners as much as cattle or buildings were.

From the time they first settled in Britain, the Saxons were threatened on all sides – either by Britons or by other groups of Saxons. So Saxon society was shaped by war. Their first leaders were popular and successful fighters, but they needed long-term support. Loyalty and service were necessary for a kingdom to survive, and a man's bonds with his lord outweighed even family ties. The tales of Saxon battles are full of the heroic loyalty of soldiers to their leaders. Bede records, for example, the story of Lilla, a servant of King Edwin of Northumbria; Lilla threw himself in front of his lord to take upon his own body the enemy blows intended for the king. It was shameful for a soldier to return from a battle in which his lord had been killed, and men followed defeated leaders into exile if they survived.

This kind of loyalty is just one example of the way Saxon society worked. They totally accepted that people of noble or royal birth were superior. It was as important in peacetime as in war for those of lower birth to do service to their lord. In this way, Saxons accepted their lord's justice, worked on his lands and paid him taxes. In return, they expected fair rule and protection from attack.

Questions

Section A

1 Write a definition of each of the following words.

   fyrd   thane   eorl
   Witan   feorms   reeve
   churls   hide   thrall

2 Draw a triangle and write KING at the top to indicate that the king was at the top of Saxon society. Then write CHURL, THRALL and THANE on your triangle, in the places you think most suitable.

3 Write in one sentence underneath the triangle why this is a suitable shape to use to represent Saxon society.

Section B

4 It is harvest time for Oswald, Astrid and their children. They need to get in the crop to feed themselves in the coming winter. How do you think they would feel if:

   a the weather was good?
   b it rained all day?
   c Oswald got a call to join his lord's army for an attack on a neighbouring kingdom?

   Explain your answers.

Activity

The Northumbrians would have admired Lilla for the way he died. Put yourself in the place of a Northumbrian and write one phrase as an epitaph for Lilla (e.g. 'He died for his country'). Then get into groups of four and choose the best epitaph in your group. Discuss *why* it is the best. The example given above is probably *not* suitable. Why not?

Life in Saxon England

The Saxons had no tradition of living in stone buildings. They didn't have the will or the skills to rebuild or repair the Roman towns and villas, and they were superstitious about the spirits or ghosts which might inhabit these stone ruins. A few early Saxon settlements were sited in the streets beside the Roman ruins, but most were farming villages among the fields.

The Britons had farmed only the upland areas of Britain, the chalk or limestone hills such as the South Downs and the Chilterns. The Saxons farmed these areas, but also axed down the thick lowland forests. They used heavy ploughs drawn by eight oxen to turn the thick soil.

The Saxons also introduced the **open-field system** of farming. This meant turning all the farmland around each village into two or three large fields and dividing them into strips of land which were shared among the villagers. This system was meant to share out the best and worst land equally. But the Saxons knew nothing about fertilisers and found that using the same land year after year led to poorer and poorer crops; so they had to leave one of the fields fallow, or unused, every year, which was very wasteful. This system of land use was to last for more than a thousand years in most areas of England.

Barley was the main crop, used to make bread and ale. Wheat, rye and oats were the other main cereals grown. Beans, peas, leeks and onions were about the Saxons' only vegetables. There was some milk, cheese and meat, but this was limited. The Saxons could not grow enough fodder to feed their livestock through the winter, and so most of the animals were killed in the **autumn slaughter**. The villages could still supply most of their needs; and they relied on travelling pedlars only for salt, to preserve the meat, and for iron, to make tools and weapons.

The typical Saxon village, or **tun**, contained a number of timber huts with thatched roofs of straw, reeds or heather. The largest, for the thane or lord, could be a 24-metre hall with benches and trestle tables along the sides for eating, and a large fire in the centre for heat and light. Followers and guests would sleep either on the benches or on the hard earth floor, which was strewn with rushes or straw. There might be a private living area for the lord and his family. Other buildings would include barns and byres, or sheds, and the huts of the churls. These were primitive wooden thatched homes, probably just a single room, sunken into the ground to make them easier to build, very dark, damp and cold.

These are the contents of a grave excavated in Kent. It contained the skeleton of a woman and the following photographed objects:

a *two small brooches with semi-circular heads;*
b *two small brooches with oblong heads;*
c *a large iron buckle;*
d *a smaller bronze buckle;*
e *two small button brooches with human faces;*
f *a silver spoon with perforated bowl;*
g *parts of an ivory charm;*
h *silver earrings with glass beads;*
i *various beads of crystal, black glass, amber and paste.*

Also in the grave were:
- *an iron knife;*
- *three coins – the latest made in about AD 470.*

Source B

14

13

A reconstruction of a Saxon home. The hut measured about 6 metres by 3.5 metres. Inside you can see an upright loom.

Life for the lord and his family included hawking and hunting, and feasts in the great hall, with minstrels, songs, sagas and plenty of mead and ale. Their clothes were made from fur or wool or fine cloth, and they wore ornamental buckles and brooches. We know from the finds at Sutton Hoo that the wealthiest Saxons owned very fine jewellery.

But life was hard and perilous for the churls. Their clothes were made from coarse linen and leather; their diet must have been poor and monotonous. Skeletons that have been found show that their living conditions produced many illnesses like rheumatism.

Slowly, some towns began to grow, especially in the South East. Saxon place-name endings, including *-burgh* or *-bury* (a fortified place), *-port* (a harbour or market) and *-chester* (an old Roman site), suggest why towns developed where they did. Trade also increased as some areas built up their resources of wool or metals. As in Roman times, ships again began to take goods back and forth across the sea to the Continent.

With the growth of trade came the need for money; some towns became minting places, licensed by kings to produce bronze, silver or gold coins. By the end of the Saxon period, in the eleventh century, towns like London, Canterbury, Winchester, Oxford, Lincoln and York had populations of between five and ten thousand inhabitants.

Questions

Section A

1 Write a brief paragraph to describe each of the following:

 a The lord's hall.   **c** The churl's diet.
 b The churl's hut.   **d** Saxon farming.

2 Match up the numbered objects in Source A with the list of objects given in the caption, e.g. Item 13 = (f) the silver spoon.

3 **a** What kind of person do you think lived in the house pictured in Source B? Give reasons for your answer.
 b What kind of person do you think was buried in the grave whose belongings are pictured in Source A? Explain your answers.

Section B

4 **a** How would you feel if you had to live in a house like Source B?
 b How would a thrall feel?
 c How would a churl feel?

Explain your answers.

Early Saxon Laws

Saxon laws were based on customs brought over from the Continent and adapted in England. They allowed a man's kindred (his relatives) to claim compensation if a crime was committed against him. The level of compensation depended on the seriousness of the crime. For example, if a man was murdered, his kindred would claim compensation according to his **wergeld**, or price. The price of a thane was 6,000 silver pence; for a churl it was 2,000 pence in Kent, 1,000 in Wessex and 800 in Mercia and Northumbria.

Britons were usually valued at half the price of a Saxon, but thralls had no wergeld; they were treated as property rather than as people. There were even wergelds for parts of the body. For other crimes, such as theft, a man and his kindred might claim compensation, or the wrongdoer could be whipped or have a hand or a foot cut off. Serious crimes such as treason against the king or the lord were punished by hanging. To escape punishment, offenders sometimes ran away. They were then declared outlaws and could be hunted and killed on sight.

If a man's kindred could not get the compensation they thought they deserved, then they would often carry out a **blood feud** against the kindred of the offender. This involved attacks and murders, and in some cases went on for generations.

Trials were held by the **ealdorman** (elder) at large open-air meetings of the village, called **folk moots**. If the person accused of the crime failed to appear, he was assumed guilty. His kindred paid the compensation, or he was declared an outlaw. If he did appear, he swore on oath that he was innocent: 'By the Lord, I am not guilty of the crime with which I am charged.' He also produced **oath-helpers**, usually his kindred; they swore: 'By the Lord, the defendant's oath is true and not false.'

The more oath-helpers there were, and the higher their rank, the more they were believed. If the oaths were convincing, the accused was cleared. If there were witnesses to a crime, the accuser would also produce oath-helpers: 'In the name of almighty God, I saw with my eyes that of which I speak.'

If the oaths seemed to show guilt, the accused had to undergo an **ordeal**, either by water or by fire. A priest would ask the accused to admit his guilt. If he refused, he might be given holy water to drink, tied up and thrown into a deep stream or pond, and if he floated he was pronounced guilty. Or he might be made to carry a red-hot iron nearly three

Source A

faxtax. Jclypoðon tophapaoner
ðinc þeopaꝛ uꝛmanne ꝛylleð
l ꞅeþeopc. nuþe þincðeopaꝛ ꝛynð
yꝛ ꞅeðon þiþðinꝼolc · Ðacꝑæð hr

Saxon punishment. The man tied up is being whipped. The man on the right is heating up a branding iron.

metres, or to plunge his hand into boiling water to pick up a stone; if three days later the wound had started to fester or became septic, then he was declared guilty.

Saxon women could own land in their own name and took part in trials as oath-helpers; but wergeld did not apply to them.

Defendants and witnesses in court-room trials are today asked to swear an oath that they will speak the truth – something passed down to us from the Saxon system. Saxon law was surprisingly effective: guilty men would be less likely to find oath-helpers, and an oath-helper who was telling lies would be less convincing. Guilt had really been established before the ordeal took place. Saxon law also had a religious aspect, because oath-helpers risked offending God if they lied. It was believed that the ordeal gave God a chance to establish innocence through holy water or fire.

Questions

Section A

1 The beginning and endings of the following sentences have been mixed up. Match the correct heads and tails.

Heads	Tails
a A man's wergeld was	his relatives who protected his rights in law.
b Folk moots were	witnesses who spoke up for the accused at his trial.
c Oath-helpers were	open-air meetings where the trials were held.
d A man's kindred were	a test to see if God confirmed the man's guilt.
e The ordeal was	his value or price in law.

Section B

2 You know the wergeld for men's lives. Make up a list to show the compensation which might have been paid in Saxon times for the loss of (a) an eye, (b) an ear, (c) an arm. Write out the reasons for your answers.

3 Get together in groups of about four. Plan and act out the trial which might have led to the punishment shown in Source A. Show what the following people would have said, done and felt: (a) the ealdorman, (b) the accuser, (c) the accused, (d) the oath-helpers.

4 When a cow disappeared from the village, Eadric, an old hermit who lived alone in the forest, was accused. Oswald, one of the lord's thralls, said that he saw Eadric steal the cow. Eadric could produce only one oath-helper at the trial, and he was forced to suffer the ordeal of fire. Unexpectedly, his wounds seemed quite clean three days later.

   a How would you explain these events now?
   b How would a Saxon villager have explained them at the time?

Christianity and the Synod of Whitby

Christianity came to Britain during the Roman occupation and remained after the Roman legions had left. The Anglo-Saxon invaders were not Christians but pagans. As the newcomers swept across most of present-day England, the Britons seem either to have let their Christian faith lapse or to have fled to Cornwall, Wales, Ireland or north-west England, taking their Christian beliefs with them.

The conversion of the English to Christianity began with **Pope Gregory**. In AD 596 he sent a Benedictine prior named **Augustine** and forty monks to spread the faith in Britain. The mission did not go well at first. Dismayed at tales of Saxon barbarity which he heard in Gaul, Augustine returned almost immediately. Gregory had to pursuade him to try again.

In 597 Augustine landed on the Isle of Thanet in the kingdom of Kent. King Ethelbert was mistrustful, but Augustine had the advantage that Ethelbert's wife, Bertha, was a Christian princess from Gaul; part of her marriage settlement had been that she was able to keep her Christian faith. Kent also had long-established contacts with Christian traders from Gaul. Ethelbert's doubts were soon overcome and he was baptised before the year was out.

The Kentish king's influence stretched over several smaller kingdoms. Bede reports: 'The king would not compel anyone to accept Christianity, but he showed greater favour to believers.' More baptisms followed amongst kings and nobles in Essex and East Anglia, and many English peasants faithfully followed the example of their rulers. In 601 Pope Gregory made Augustine Archbishop of Canterbury, head of the Church of Britain, and bishops were installed in Rochester and London.

This success was short-lived. Gregory died in 604; Augustine died soon after. In 616 King Ethelbert died, and his successor was not Christian. Other Christian kings either renounced their faith or were followed by pagan kings. The bishops were expelled from Rochester and London.

In 627 another monk, Paulinus, was sent by the Pope to Northumbria. A pagan king there, Edwin, had married a Christian daughter of Ethelbert and he was converted. Again, large numbers of his people followed suit. However, when Edwin was killed in battle in 633, by the pagan King Penda of Mercia, this was said to be a sign of the anger of the pagan gods. The conversions stopped. Monks remained in Kent, but the spread of Christianity from the South had halted.

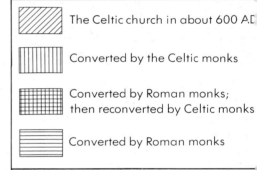

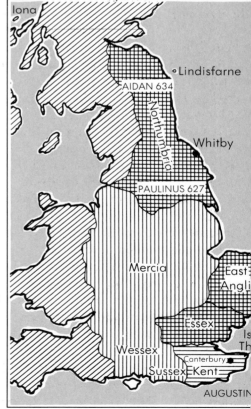

The conversion of the English.

A Celtic cross. These crosses were made in wood and then stone by the Celtic monks wherever they regularly preached before they could manage to build a church. They were erected all over the north of England.

The revival came from the North. Christianity had survived strongly in the Celtic Church – among the Britons of Wales, Ireland and Scotland – since the Anglo-Saxon invasions. In 634 **Aidan** and twelve other Celtic monks travelled from their monastery in Iona to try to bring Christianity back to Northumbria. They set up a mission on the island of Lindisfarne, and although they had the support of King Oswald they preached among the ordinary people. Their following grew. Even when Oswald was killed in battle by the fierce King Penda in 641, the conversions contined. The Christian influence of the monks spread southwards into Mercia, East Anglia and Wessex, gradually reaching all of the English kingdoms.

The Celtic Church had developed its own customs, which were different from the teachings of the Roman missionaries in Kent. The Celtic and Roman Churches celebrated Easter at different dates. More serious, the Celtic abbots and bishops had refused to accept the Archbishop of Canterbury, appointed by the Pope in Rome, as the head of the whole Christian Church in Britain. They had grown used to more freedom and wanted to keep it.

It was illogical to have two groups of Christians – Celtic and Roman – worshipping the same God and working side by side but using different customs. Something had to be done. **King Oswy** of Northumbria was England's most powerful king at that time. In 664 Oswy called a **synod**, or council, of Church leaders at Whitby. Not all of the differences could be removed at once, but most of the Celtic priests agreed on a new date for Easter and accepted the leadership of the Pope. After the Synod of Whitby the Church became more unified.

Questions

Section A

1 Draw a time-line of the events in this unit.

2 Write briefly about each of the following people: Gregory, Augustine, Ethelbert, Aidan, Oswy.

Section B

3 Write a list of five reasons why Augustine's mission to England was such a great success at first.

4 Write a list of four reasons why the conversion of the English by Augustine in Kent and by Paulinus in Northumbria failed.

5 These reasons are the *causes* of success and failure. Put them together and then divide them into:

   a causes controlled by people;
   b causes beyond the control of people.

6 'Augustine's mission was doomed to fail.' Do you agree? Use your answers to questions 3, 4 and 5 in your answer.

7 Why was the Celtic conversion from the North so successful?

The Viking Raids

The people of Scandinavia – that is, Sweden, Norway and Denmark – began to explore, raid and then invade the countries around them from about AD 750. They were known as the Vikings or Northmen.

The first Viking raids on Britain's coasts were for food and riches. Then bigger attacks started to come, reaching inland. Later there was widespread invasion by large armies in search of land.

The sources that follow give a picture of these Viking attacks.

Primary sources

Source A

'AD 789. In this year came first three ships of Norsemen: and the reeve rode there and tried to compel them to go to the royal manor: and they slew him. These were the first ships of the Danes to come to England.'

From 'The Anglo-Saxon Chronicle'.

(You may find it useful to refer to The Saxons 3.1, 3.2 and 3.3, 'Who Were the Saxons?' for information about *The Anglo-Saxon Chronicle*.)

Source B

Source C

'The heathens poured out the blood of saints around the altar, and trampled on the bodies of saints in the temple of God, like dung in the streets.'

From the description by Alcuin (an English monk) of the Viking raid on the monastery at Lindisfarne, 793.

Source D

'Their army raided here and there and filled every place with bloodshed and sorrow. Far and wide they destroyed the churches and monasteries with fire and sword. When it departed it left nothing standing but roofless walls.'

Written by Simeon of Durham, an English monk, 856.

Source E

'From the terror of the Northmen, good Lord deliver us.'

From a ninth-century English prayer.

A Viking ship found at Gokstad in Norway. Its owner had been buried in it with food, drink, pots and pans, a sledge and many other articles, including a chess set for entertainment in the afterlife!

A historian would first *evaluate* the primary sources and then *use* them to build up a picture of the Viking raids.

Secondary sources

Source F

'These men of Norway and Denmark found it hard to keep their families by fishing and farming the infertile slopes of the fiords. Instead they set out to rob the wealthy monasteries and villages of England. Their dragon ships glided smoothly along the coast, then the warriors leapt quickly ashore and began their work of killing, looting and burning. Then they made a quick getaway before the Saxons could raise an army to meet them.'

From Valerie E. Chancellor, 'Medieval and Tudor Britain' (Penguin, 1970).

Source G

'[The Vikings] were a strange mixture, both savage and yet civilised. Very skilful as soldiers, sailors and farmers, they were also very vain. They bathed frequently, changed their clothes often, combed out their long golden hair and delighted in wearing silks, soft furs, fine linen and jewellery of silver and gold. Yet in battle they were wild to the point of madness, burning and killing for pleasure even defenceless women and children. In particular they delighted in robbing and destroying churches and monasteries.'

From John Bareham, 'Changing World History' (Holmes McDougall, 1976).

Source H

'They believed that only men who were killed in battle went to Valhalla, their heaven, and so they almost welcomed death, and it is thought that they chewed a highly poisonous toadstool called fly agaric, which sent them berserk, or fighting mad, before battle.'

From Peter Moss, 'History Alive, 55 BC – 1485' (Hart-Davis Educational, 1977).

Questions

Section A

1 Who were the Vikings and what lands did they come from?

2 Describe a typical Viking attack on an English coastal village.

Section B

3 a Secondary sources are based on primary sources. Can you find any statements in Source F which are *not* supported by the primary sources given in this unit?
   b Does this mean that these statements are untrue?

4 a From which type of primary sources do we get our information about the behaviour of the Vikings on their raids?
   b Are these sources likely to be fair, or could they be biased?
   c Have we any other primary evidence which gives a different picture of the character of the Vikings?

5 How much do the secondary sources show these two sides of the Vikings?

6 'The Vikings were a cruel and barbaric race.' Do you agree? Use all the evidence available to you in your answer.

Alfred and the Vikings

The Viking attacks on the English and Scottish kingdoms began at the end of the eighth century and gradually changed from raids to invasions. The monasteries at Lindisfarne and Jarrow were attacked and robbed in 793 and 794. From then on, the size and number of raids grew steadily. The first mass attack, on the Thames estuary, was in 835.

In the year 851 *The Anglo-Saxon Chronicle* reported: 'For the first time the heathen men stayed through the winter.'

In 865 Vikings from Demark who were now based in England assembled a **'Great Army'**. Led by Ivar the Boneless and his brother Halfdan, these Danes spent the winter in part of East Anglia. In 866 they conquered Northumbria. This may have been an act of revenge, because King Ella of Northumbria had killed Ivar's father by throwing him into a pit of snakes. Three years later Ivar conquered East Anglia. The Saxon king there, Edmund, would not accept Ivar's rule. He was tied to a tree and shot with arrows.

Wessex was England's richest kingdom. The Great Army attacked it in 871. The men of Wessex fought nine battles against the Danes in 871. They lost their king, Ethelred, in the spring but they fought strongly enough to hold the invaders back. Ethelred's successor was Alfred, who became king of Wessex at the age of twenty-two.

Alfred forced the Danes to give up their hopes of conquering Wessex, and he was able to pay them to leave his kingdom. The Great Army spent the winter in London and then went north, conquering Mercia. Some of them, under Halfdan, settled in Northumbria. Wessex was safe for a few years.

But Alfred was not idle. An entry in *The Anglo-Saxon Chronicle* says that a Danish fleet was sighted off the south coast in 875. This probably happened often in those years. The *Chronicle* then adds: 'King Alfred went out to sea with a navy and fought against the crews of seven ships. He captured one ship and put the rest to flight.'

This is the first record of an organised navy defending England since Roman times. It must have given the Danes quite a shock.

In the winter of 876–7 Guthrum, the new leader of the Vikings, unexpectedly attacked Chippenham. The people of Wessex were still celebrating Christmas, and most of the army had been disbanded. Alfred had only a bodyguard of about two hundred soldiers with him. Wessex was overrun and fell under Danish control as far west as Selwood.

This was the lowest point of English fortunes. Alfred went

Danish lands in England, about 900 AD.

into hiding in the marshlands around the Isle of Athelney, in Somerset. He never lost hope, sending messages to his people to prepare for revenge. By May 877, reassured by messages of support, he was able to slip out of hiding.

Source A

'Alfred rode to Egbert's Stone and came to meet him there all the men of Somerset and Wiltshire and part of Hampshire and they rejoiced to see him. And he went … to Edington and there he fought against the entire host, and put it to flight.'

From 'The Anglo-Saxon Chronicle'.

Alfred's victory over the Danes in 877 at Edington brought about lasting peace. Guthrum agreed to leave Wessex, was baptised into the Christian Church with twenty-nine of his followers, and retreated to East Anglia to settle his troops. Only once, in 885, did he seriously break this treaty, when a Danish force attacking from the Continent tempted him to support them. But Alfred beat off the invaders and took back a large area of central and eastern England, including London, from Guthrum as a punishment.

Alfred and Guthrum made a new treaty in 886. This agreement showed exactly the area of eastern England which was to remain under Danish rule. This area, called the **Danelaw**, is marked on the map, and is the subject of The Saxons 3.13.

Only one more period of Danish attacks, from 892 to 896, worried Alfred's reign, but this was never a serious threat. Alfred had again used the peaceful years wisely. He had strengthened his navy, building ships that were rowed by sixty oars and were almost twice the size of the Danish ships. Under Alfred's orders, a series of fortified towns called burghs were built (see The Saxons 3.12, Sources C–E).

Alfred also reorganised the army. The Saxon army or **fyrd** had always suffered from being a temporary fighting force. It was made up of untrained peasants who would often return to their fields at harvest times. Alfred divided his army into two parts, releasing one half to work on their land and keeping the other as a permanent standing army, swapping them over at intervals.

In this way Wessex survived the Danish storm which ravaged the rest of the country although Alfred never tried to drive the Danes from eastern England. Because of his successes and the destruction of the other kingdoms, by the time of his death in the year 900, he was accepted as the ruler of all England outside of the Danelaw.

Questions

Section A

1 Draw a time-line and mark on it the events of the Danish attacks.

2 Draw graph like the one below. Mark on it the high and low points of Alfred's struggle against the Great Army. Label each point on the graph.

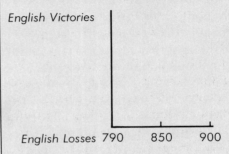

English Victories

English Losses 790   850   900

Section B

3 In what ways did King Alfred strengthen the defences of Wessex and England?

4 a Rearrange the list of events given below into chronological order:

The battle at Edington.
The first winter the Danes stayed in England.
The Danelaw.
Guthrum's attack on Chippenham.
The raid on Lindisfarne.
The Great Army of 865 arrives.

b Write a paragraph which includes all of the events and explains the connections between them.

The Reign of King Alfred

We saw in the last unit how King Alfred successfully defended Wessex against the Viking Danes. But Alfred was a remarkable man in many other ways.

Alfred worked very hard to improve and strengthen his kingdom. He wrote a new set of laws for the country, probably because the old system was not working very well. He thought that education was important for the future of his people and did much to encourage learning. At Alfred's court a school was set up for royal and noble children. Leading scholars came to the court to study and to teach.

The king also set about educating himself. At the age of forty he learned Latin and translated several books, including one by Pope Gregory which explained how priests should look after people. He was the only king before Henry VIII who wrote books. It was probably Alfred who ordered *The Anglo-Saxon Chronicle* to be started.

Alfred was a moral man. His older brother left two sons, who were Alfred's rivals for the throne. There are many examples in history of kings murdering or exiling such rivals; but Alfred treated these two kindly, and they became his willing helpers.

Source A

'Then I, King Alfred, collected these laws together and ordered to be written many which our forefathers kept, which I liked; and many of those which I did not like I rejected with the advice of my councillors. But I dared not presume to set in writing many laws of my own, because it was unknown to me what would please those who should come after us.'

'Let each man carefully keep any promise which he makes.'

'We command that the man who knows his enemy to be at home is not to fight before he has asked him to do justice.'

'If anyone disturbs a folk-moot by drawing his sword, he is to pay 120 shillings to the ealdorman as a fine.'

'Whoever steals on Sunday or at Christmas or Easter, is to pay double compensation for his theft.'

From King Alfred's laws, 'The Dooms of Alfred'.

Source B

'I remembered I had seen, before it was all attacked and burnt up, how the churches throughout all England stood filled with treasures and books. Wise councillors there were of old, and how happy were those times then, and how the kings maintained peace, morals and authority. Strangers came to these lands in search of wisdom, and now we must get these things from abroad. So utterly is learning fallen off that there are few who understand their [church] service books.'

'All the youth which now is in England, who have wealth enough to be able to apply themselves to it, be set to learning, till the time that they can read anything written in English. Let those who can be taught further be set apart for a higher office and be taught Latin.'

'You nobles judge badly because you pretend to be wise, but really you are ignorant. Unless you go to school and learn wisdom, you must give up being a judge.'

From King Alfred's writings on education.

Source C

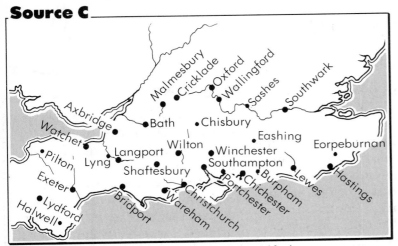

Sites of the burghs (fortified towns) built by Alfred.

Source D

Aerial view of Wallingford, one of Alfred's burghs. The lines of the walls can be clearly seen.

Source E

The remains of the earth walls built to defend one of Alfred's burghs, Wareham in Dorset.

Questions

Section A

1 Why do you think it was so important for Alfred to sort out the country's laws and send his new ones everywhere?

2 a How did Alfred encourage education in Wessex?
b Why would education and learning benefit his people?

3 Is it fair to say that Alfred was a moral and religious king?

4 Is there enough evidence to show that Alfred was a good organiser?

Section B

5 a List as many ways as you can in which Alfred was typical of his times.
b List as many things about Alfred as you can which were not typical.
c Was Alfred a typical Anglo-Saxon? Explain your answer.

6 In about 895 a small group of Danish ships were raiding the coast around the Isle of Wight. Alfred sent nine of his ships against them. He was proud of these ships; they were bigger than any the Danes had. The English ships blockaded the Danes in Southampton Water, but were caught out by the different tides and ran aground. To make things worse, three of the stranded English ships were cut off from the others, and the Danes were able to attack them and kill the crew. The smaller Danish vessels were able to sail away before the English ones could be refloated.

a This story shows that Alfred's navy was useless. Do you agree?
b Does this story tell us anything about the role of wartime leaders like Alfred?

7 Alfred is the only English king who is called the 'Great'.

a Do you think he earned this title?
b What difference do you think it might have made to the later history of England if Alfred had died before he became king?

71

The Danelaw

The Danes had defeated the rulers of Northumbria, Mercia and East Anglia. King Alfred signed a treaty with Guthrum, the leader of the Viking invaders. This agreement allowed the Danes to rule an area of England, to be called the Danelaw, stretching north-east from a line drawn roughly between London and Liverpool, as far north as the river Tees. Most of the Viking warriors settled there as farmers and adopted the Christian beliefs of the English.

Alfred's successors gradually managed to reconquer the Danelaw, although the Danish settlers continued to live there.

Historians have not been able to answer some questions about the Danelaw. For example:

- How many Danes settled in the Danelaw?
- Exactly where did they settle?
- How did the Danes treat the English they settled among?

The accounts of the Danish settlements given in Sources A and B both agree on some basic information about the settlement. But they give different pictures of what the Danelaw was like.

Source A

'The Great Army of Danes put their own leader on the throne of Northumbria and half of them settled in Yorkshire. After terrorising the Midlands, another section of the Great Army colonised Lincolnshire, Nottinghamshire, Derbyshire and Leicestershire. After King Alfred of Wessex defeated the Great Army in 878, Guthrum was recognised as the king of eastern and northern England, and the rest of his men settled in East Anglia.

'In the Danelaw, the Danish soldiers quickly established a society of their own. Their impact was startling and this shows the army was very large. Even when the Danes became Christians and were reconquered by Alfred's successors, the area covered by the Danelaw remained very different from the rest of England.'

Source B

'After campaigns which took them over large areas of the country, small groups of Danes settled on land not previously occupied by the English, mainly in Leicestershire, Lincolnshire, Nottinghamshire and East Yorkshire, and to a lesser extent in East Anglia. There were not enough of them to swamp the existing English population and they lived in peaceful coexistence, continuing to speak their own language and influencing local customs.'

Source C

The English language now contains many words of Scandinavian origin. These include many everyday words like 'husband', 'window', 'knife', 'fellow', 'sky', 'skin', 'ugly', 'happy', 'loose', 'wrong', 'leg', 'take', 'call', 'hit', 'anger', 'low', 'though', 'root' and 'they', 'them' and 'their'. There are also many Scandinavian-derived words to do with the legal system and government, like 'law' and 'outlaw'.

The shaded area shows where place-names of Scandinavian origin are common; these usually end in '-by' or '- thorpe' or '-toft'. The darker shading shows where most of these names are to be found. Anglo-Saxon place names have not been completely replaced. There is evidence that the places marked by names of Scandinavian origin were the areas of less fertile soil, whereas the Anglo-Saxon settlements were in the better farming areas.

From K.O. Morgan, 'The Oxford Illustrated History of England' (Oxford University Press, 1984).

From Ralph Arnold, 'A Social History of England from 55 BC to AD 1215' (Longman, 1967).

Source D

Southern limit
of Danelaw

Northumberland	16 Lincolnshire
Tyne & Wear	17 Staffordshire
Durham	18 Leicestershire
Cleveland	19 Norfolk
Cumbria	20 West Midlands
North Yorkshire	21 Warwickshire
West Yorkshire	22 Northamptonshire
South Yorkshire	23 Cambridgeshire
Humberside	24 Suffolk
Lancashire	25 Bedfordshire
Merseyside	26 Buckinghamshire
Greater Manchester	27 Hertfordshire
Cheshire	28 Essex
Derbyshire	29 Greater London
Nottinghamshire	

Next, to help you decide what *your own* view of these questions is, consider the evidence in Sources C – F.

Source E

The Domesday Book (see The Normans 4.4) was a survey of all the land in England, made in 1086. Counties in the South were divided into 'hundreds' for local government and the law. But the counties in the North were divided into *wapentakes* (a Danish word). Yorkshire was treated as three separate counties, each part being called a *thrithing*, (Danish for a third), which we now call the Yorkshire Ridings.

Also in the Domesday Book, there were differences in the way **farmland** was measured. In the southern counties, the farms were measured in 'hides' (a number of acres which varied from place to place) and 'yardlands' (one-quarter of a hide). But in the North they were divided into 'ploughlands' (the area which one plough-team could plough in a year) and 'bovates' (one-eighth of a ploughland).

Source F

The Anglo-Saxon Chronicle refers to the Danish soldiers as the 'Micel Here', the Great Army, but it never tells us how many people were actually in it. The military victories suggest large numbers, but it would have been impossible to supply many thousands of men for so many years, and the Viking ships probably carried only about thirty-five at a time. Danes arriving in England after the establishment of the Danelaw are likely to have been settlers rather than soldiers.

Questions

Section A

1 Draw a table to compare what the two accounts say about:

   a the numbers of Danish settlers.
   b the exact location of the Danish settlements.
   c how peacefully the Danes settled in, and what their relationship with the English was like.

Section B

2 What does the evidence given in Sources C – F suggest about:

   a the number of Danish settlers?
   b the exact place of the Danish settlements?
   c how the Danes and the existing English inhabitants behaved towards each other?

3 Write your own description of the Danelaw. Use all your ideas from question 2 and back up your opinions with evidence from Sources C – F.

4 Compare your version of events in the Danelaw with other people's. You probably will not find any other accounts quite like yours. Why is this? Does it mean that your account is wrong?

How England Became United

The kings of Wessex who followed Alfred gradually won control over the Danelaw. So they became the first kings of all England, though they also had more Viking raids to cope with. The sources below (some are primary and some are secondary) give details of all the main events, but they are muddled. Your job – the job historians often have to do – is to make sense of this jumble of information.

Source A

'AD 937. Never before on this island … was a greater slaughter of a host made by the edge of a sword since the Angles and Saxons came here.'

'The Anglo-Saxon Chronicle' reporting on victory in the North at Brunanburh by Athelstan, grandson of King Alfred, over a combined army of Scots, Britons and Norsemen. This gave Athelstan control of all England, and he began to call himself 'Rex Totius Britannae' (King of All Britain) on his coins.

Source B

'AD 980. Southampton was ransacked by a naval force, and in the same year Thanet was ravaged.'

★ ★ ★ ★ ★

'AD 981. Three ships of Vikings arrived in Dorset and ravaged in Portland. This same year London was burnt down.'

'The Anglo-Saxon Chronicle' reporting new Viking attacks on England by small groups of adventurers. Strong Scandinavian kings were soon to follow, with large well-trained armies, hoping to conquer land.

Source C

'When the enemy were in the east, the English army was in the west, and when they were in the south, our army was in the north.'

From 'The Anglo-Saxon Chronicle' during the reign of Ethelred the Unready, king of England from AD 975 to 1016.

Source D

'Byrhtnoth spoke; he grasped his shield;
… Resolute, he uttered these words in reply,
"Viking herald, return with our answer:
Here unafraid an eorl stands with his troops,
Who will defend his native land,
The realm of Ethelred, my prince." '

From a poem, 'The Battle of Maldon', AD 991. The poem goes on to tell how Byrhtnoth's army was slaughtered. The king decided to bribe the Vikings to leave with a large payment of money, called the Danegeld. He had to make more payments of Danegeld between 991 and 1012 to keep Viking raiders away.

Source E

A coin from Ethelred's reign. Thousands of these were found all over Scandinavia.

74

Source F

The name Ethelred means 'good counsel', or good advice. Because he failed to hold back the Vikings, the king was nicknamed 'Unred', which means badly advised or unadvised – Ethelred the Unred. This name came down to us as Ethelred the Unready.

Source G

'Athelstan, AD 924 – 939, was the first king of all England. But his successors, Edmund, Edred, and Edwig, had to carry on the fight. It was not until the reign of Edgar, AD 959 – 975, that there was any long period of peace; with it came a great rebuilding of monasteries, of education and arts, to bring the seeds of Alfred's work to fruition.'

From R. Cramp and J. Gummer, 'The Earliest English' (Edward Arnold, 1963).

Source H

'Alfred's successors made rapid headway from 910. Edward of Wessex and the Lady Ethelfleda of Mercia, his sister, began to push eastwards. In 916 Bedford submitted, in the following year Derby, and in 918 Colchester, Northampton and Leicester. On Ehtelfreda's death, in the same year, Edward took over Mercia, and by 920 the Danes of York and East Anglia had acknowledged him as overlord. The rule of the House of Wessex now stretched over the whole of Southern England and the Midlands.'

From R.R. Sellman, 'The Vikings' (Methuen, 1957).

Source I

'Finally, Swein "Forkbeard", king of Denmark, decided to conquer England. In 1013 he landed with a large army. Ethelred fled and Swein took the crown. He was only king for a few weeks. He collapsed and died in February 1014. Ethelred came back but was soon faced with an army led by Swein's son, Cnut (sometimes spelt Canute), and by the end of 1016, Ethelred was dead and the English had to accept Cnut, the king of Denmark, as the king of England too.'

From R.J. Cootes, 'The Middle Ages' (Longman 1972).

Source J

'Cnut died in 1035. Seven years later, his only two sons were dead too. The Witan summoned Edward, Ethelred's son, back from exile in Normandy to become king. Edward, the great-great-great-grandson of King Alfred, was king until 1066.'

Notes taken by a pupil in a modern history lesson.

Questions

Section A

1 Sources A, B and C are all taken from *The Anglo-Saxon Chronicle*. Does this mean either that all three must be true or that all three must be false? Explain your answer.

2 Source D is a poem. Can a poem be a reliable source for historians? Give reasons for your answer.

3 Is each of the following sources primary or secondary for a historian studying England between AD 900 and 1066: Source A? Source F? Source G? Source J?

4 Why might a historian think that Source E is a very important source to show how weak England was in the early eleventh century?

Section B

5 Make a list of the reigns of English kings in chronological order (the order in which they happened). Start with Alfred, AD 871 – 900, and note the ones who were king of *all* England. Give the dates of their reigns where you can.

6 Draw a time-line to show what happened betwen AD 900 and 1066.

7 Using your list of kings and your time-line to help you, write a short account of the history of England between the death of Alfred and the reign of Edward the Confessor.

8 Do you think *one year* during that time was more important than all the others? If so, which one and why? If you don't think any one year was more important, explain why you think this.

Background to the Norman Conquest

Harold of Wessex and the battle of Stamford Bridge

As the year 1066 began, England's king, Edward the Confessor, was an old and sick man. He had been king since 1042. No one expected him to live much longer. Edward had no children and no surviving brothers or sisters.

Who would be the next king? **Prince Edgar** was the king's nearest blood relative, and so had a good claim on the throne. He was descended from Alfred the Great and was Edward's nephew's son. But Edgar was only a child, with no experience of government or war.

Edward died on 5 January. On his deathbed, he named **Harold Godwin**, Earl of Wessex, to succeed him. The leading nobles gathered in the Witan, the king's advisory council, and confirmed the choice.

Harold had been the leader of the king's army. He had already driven off an invasion by the King of Wales in 1063. As the Earl of Wessex, he had governed part of England; and because his sister Edith had been Edward's wife, he was related to the royal family by marriage. On 7 January, King Harold was crowned at Westminster Abbey, like every English monarch ever since.

However, **Duke William of Normandy**, was angry. He had visited England in 1051 and he claimed that King Edward had promised him the throne. Also, Harold had been to Normandy in 1064. Whilst he was there, William said, Harold had sworn an oath on a box of holy relics, promising to help him get the throne. William prepared to invade England.

A third man claimed the English throne. He was **Harold Hardrada**, King of Norway. He said that, before the Saxon Edward the Confessor, the Viking warrior Cnut had been King of England from 1016 to 1035. Then Cnut's two Viking sons had shared the throne until 1042. If there was no obvious Saxon ruler, Hardrada argued, then the throne should go back to one of the Danish kings. Hardrada had the support of a large army and of Harold Godwin's brother Tostig, who had quarrelled with the new king and now wanted revenge. They prepared to invade too.

By August 1066, Duke William was ready to sail from Normandy. King Harold gathered his army and stationed them along the south coast to await the attack. All through the summer Harold's fleet lay off the Isle of Wight, guarding

Source A

A section of the Bayeux Tapestry. The words on the tapestry say: 'Harold made a sacred oath to Duke William.'

the Channel. But the northerly winds kept William in the port of St Valéry, and the months dragged by. Then, on 8 September, Harold was forced to disband his army. They had their harvest to collect, and Harold could feed them no longer. He sent his fleet back to winter on the Thames.

Two disasters quickly followed. First, the English fleet was caught in gales in the Channel, and many ships were wrecked. Then, on 18 September, Hardrada and Tostig landed in the Humber Estuary with an invasion fleet of 300 ships. King Harold's earls in the north - Morcar, Earl of Mercia, and his brother Edwin, Earl of Northumbria - marched from York to meet the invaders. The English army was defeated at the battle of Fulford on 20 September. Hardrada controlled the North.

Harold hurried north with his housecarls, a highly trained bodyguard, gathering other forces along the 190 mile route. He made very fast progress. On the morning of 25 September he surprised Hardrada's troops as they rested at Stamford Bridge, just outside York. In an unusually bloody battle, the invading army was slaughtered. Hardrada and Tostig were both killed, and so few others survived that only twenty-four of the original 300 ships were needed to ferry them home.

King Harold had seen off one challenge, but only three days later the winds changed. On 28 September, William's invasion fleet left Normandy.

Questions

Section A

1 Draw up a chart to explain the situation in 1066, using these headings: The claimant; His claim to the throne; The strongest aspect of this claim; The weakest aspect of this claim.

2 The Bayeux Tapestry was made in Normandy after 1066. It showed Harold promising to help William get the throne after Edward (see Source A). Do you think Harold broke this promise?

3 Who do you think had the strongest claim to the throne when Edward died? Explain your answer.

Section B

4 Here is a list of the first kings of England:

924 – 939	Athelstan	Saxon
939 – 946	Edmund	Saxon
946 – 955	Eadred	Saxon
955 – 959	Eadwig	Saxon
959 – 975	Edgar	Saxon
975 – 1016	Ethelred	Saxon
1016 – 1034	Cnut	Viking
1034 – 1042	Cnut's sons	Viking
1042 – 1066	Edward the Confessor	Saxon

a Put these reigns on a pie chart. Remembering that Hardrada was a Viking, does your diagram give you any idea of the strength of Hardrada's claim to the throne?

b Draw another pie chart showing the English kings, but this time start at 1016. What idea does this diagram give of the strength of Hardrada's claim.

c What do diagrams a and b tell us about the way that time-scales affect our view of events?

Source B

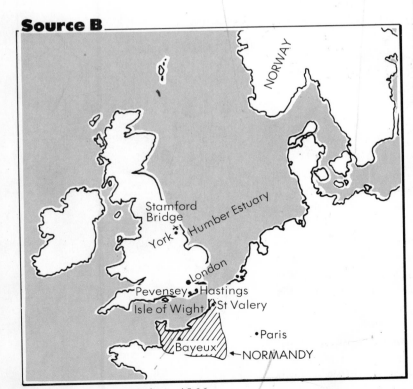

England and Normandy in 1066.

The Battle of Hastings

Duke William of Normandy set sail across the Channel on 28 September 1066. He had 696 ships and an army of about 7,000 soldiers including many archers and horsemen. The crossing was made dangerous by the uncertain tides and weather. The Norman force also ran the risk of being attacked by Harold's fleet or of being surprised by his army while landing on the beaches. However, William's men made a safe landing at Pevensey, near Hastings, the next morning.

King Harold probably heard of William's landing on 1 October. He decided on the same tactics which had worked so well against Hardrada—a surprise attack. He marched the 190 miles back to London so fast that the majority of his army, already weakened by battle, were left far behind. Without waiting for reinforcements, Harold marched the further sixty miles to the south coast. He arrived with about 7,000 men too, although only about 2,000 of these were his highly trained housecarls. The rest were peasants from the surrounding districts, so Harold had few archers or horsemen.

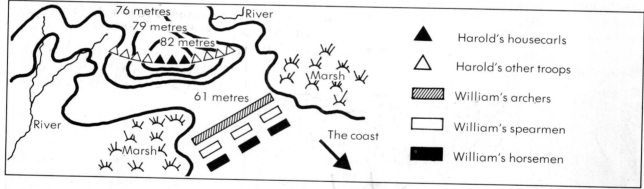

The positions of the two armies at the Battle of Hastings.

By the evening of 13 October, the English army was still seven miles short of the Norman forces. Whilst the army rested overnight, William's scouts reported their position. William began to get his men ready, and he roused them at four o'clock the next morning.

Harold also prepared carefully for the battle. He drew up his soldiers on the top of a ridge which had marshes on both sides. This forced the Normans to attack uphill on a narrow front. The Norman horsemen were unable to make quick attacks, and the Saxon troops could defend themselves behind a wall of shields at the top of the slope.

The fighting began at about nine o'clock, lasting most of the day. The Norman attacks had little effect at first. In the words of a Norman who was not at the battle but who later became one of William's trusted officials:

'Our soldiers attacked, hurling spears and javelins at the English. They resisted bravely and returned the fire with spears, axes and stones. Our knights crashed into the enemy shields, but the English remained on high ground, keeping close order, and pushed our knights down the hill.'

It is not clear what broke the deadlock. The Norman account suggests that at one point the attackers began to retreat, fearing that William had been killed. Then, suddenly, 'William stood boldly in front of those in flight. "Look at me well. I am still alive and I shall yet be the victor." He restored our courage, and the knights turned to face the following English and cut them down.'

The writer goes on to suggest that the Normans learned from this:

'They remembered this trick of retreating and pretended to flee. Several thousand English quickly gave pursuit. The Normans suddenly turned their horses, surrounded the enemy and cut them down. Twice this trick was employed and at last the English tired.'

It is also possible that the death of King Harold ruined the Saxon discipline. In an account written by a Saxon monk many years later, we read: 'The enemy's army made little impression on them until, after a great slaughter on both sides, the king, alas, fell.'

The **Bayeux Tapestry** shows the death of Harold. Under the words 'Harold rex interfectus est' (King Harold is killed), one Saxon is seen pulling an arrow from his eye and another is ridden down by a knight on horseback. It is not clear which of the Saxons is Harold.

Source B

This is how the Bayeux Tapestry records Harold's death. The words say: 'Here King Harold is killed.'

Whatever the cause, by dusk the Saxons were in full retreat, Harold lay dead behind them. William was the victor.

Source A

This shows William raising his helmet to reassure his men that he is still alive. The words say: 'Here is Duke William.'

Questions

Section A

1 a Use the written sources and the Bayeux Tapestry to make a list of the weapons and equipment of the two sides.
  b Was one side armed and equipped better than the other?

2 How do you think Harold died? Use the sources in this chapter to come to an opinion and then argue a case for it.

Section B

3 List some of the reasons for William's victory, using the headings below:

  a Harold's mistakes.
  b William's actions and tactics.
  c William's good luck.

4 Divide into groups of four and discuss the following statements. You must come to an agreed comment on each one.

  a Harold fought well; he could have done no more; he was doomed to lose.
  b William had the better troops and luck on his side; he was bound to win.

5 Why do you think William won the battle of Hastings?

William Completes the Conquest

Victory at Hastings did not mean that William immediately became king. He had killed Harold, but not yet conquered England.

First, William decided to secure the Channel port of Dover. It had a strong castle which could have held out for months, but so daunting was the reputation of the fierce 'Conqueror' that the men of Dover gave up without a fight. The Normans marched on towards London, leaving a trail of destruction as they went. They stole food, burned property and killed many Saxon English. Crossing the Thames at Wallingford, William reached Berkhamsted. There, *The Anglo-Saxon Chronicle* tells us:

'He was met by Prince Edgar, Earl Edwin, Earl Morcar and all the best men from London, who submitted.'

Part of the Bayeux Tapestry showing Norman soldiers before the Battle of Hastings. The words read: 'Here is a house being burned.'

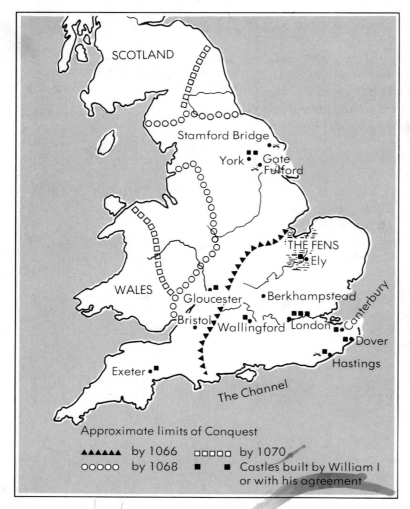

Approximate limits of Conquest

▲▲▲▲▲▲ by 1066   ◻◻◻◻◻ by 1070
○○○○○ by 1068   ■   ■ Castles built by William I or with his agreement

Norman soldiers looting a farm.

The stages of the Norman Conquest.

Thus William marched unopposed into London. On Christmas Day 1066 he was crowned William I of England.

Apart from in the South East, he was king in name only. The Norman leaders took for themselves the land of the wealthy Saxons. They increased the taxes that poorer people had to pay. The result was that William spent most of the next five years putting down revolts by the English.

One rebellion took place in Exeter, led by Harold's mother and two sons. William took hostages from the surrounding villages and demanded surrender, but still the town resisted, saying: 'We shall not swear an oath of fidelity to the pretended king, nor admit him within our walls.'

William was furious. Dragging the hostages before the city walls, he ordered one of them to be blinded. But rather than frightening the inhabitants, this act only angered them. The Normans stormed the city time and time again for eighteen days before some of the English nobles betrayed it. William took no revenge, but left soldiers to hold the town and build a castle. He then took Bristol and Gloucester. By summer 1068, he controlled the South West.

The North proved more troublesome. In the autumn of 1069, King Swein of Denmark sent a fleet of 240 ships to support an English rising at York. This revolt was led by Prince Edgar, who had returned from exile in Scotland. William's castle in York was burnt to the ground; the Norman soldiers were massacred. Hurrying north from London, William bribed the Danes not to interfere and then took the city by storm. Again the leaders of the rebellion escaped, but this time William showed no mercy. A Norman writer recorded the cruelty of his revenge:

'Never had William shown so great a cruelty. He assembled crops, herds and flocks, food and utensils of every kind and burned them all. All sources of life north of the Humber were destroyed. There followed a famine so serious that more than 100,000 of all ages and both sexes perished.'

This was the 'harrying' (destruction) of the North, the greatest stain on the reputation of the Conqueror. But it didn't bring William's troubles to an end.

In the Fens of East Anglia many of the English stubbornly resisted Norman rule. They took refuge on 'islands' like the Isle of Ely, amidst marshes which were impossible to cross except by secret tracks. These rebels were led by Hereward the Wake, who attracted other Saxon leaders like Morcar and Edwin to the Fens. Twice William launched unsuccessful raids, but in 1071 the Normans found a way through the marshes. The Fenland strongholds were overrun.

This time there was no revenge. Hereward escaped but was never heard of again. Morcar was taken prisoner. His brother Edwin was murdered by traitors among his own followers. With Edgar in exile in Scotland, no English leader ever again emerged to challenge the rule of William I.

Questions

Section A

1 Briefly say what resistance William met and how he dealt with it at each of these places: **a** Dover, **b** London, **c** Exeter, **d** York, **e** The Fens.

2 Give three reasons to explain why the English struggled for so long to resist Norman rule.

Section B

3 Draw a time-line which shows the events of the Norman Conquest. Use units 4.1, 4.2, and 4.3.

4 When did William conquer England, in 1066, 1068, 1069, 1071 or none of these? Explain your answer.

5 Sometimes a person's character shapes how much they achieve. William could be a cruel man.

  a Did he ever benefit from his reputation for cruelty?
  b Did cruelty ever fail to work for him?
  c Did his reputation for cruelty ever cause him harm?
  d Overall, do you think that his cruelty helped him or harmed him?

The Domesday Book

King William spent Christmas of 1085 at Gloucester, surrounded by his advisers. It had not been a good year. There was a constant threat of invasion from Denmark, and he had been forced to bring large numbers of knights over from Normandy at great expense to guard against attack. *The Anglo-Saxon Chronicle* tells us that William had:

'... much thought and very deep speech with his Witan about this country, how it was peopled and with what sort of men, how much land each man had and what payments were due to the king.'

There had been many changes in the ownership of land since the Conquest. William could not be sure how much tax he could raise or how many knights he was due from landowners. So, in 1086, he ordered a nation-wide survey to find out exactly who owned land in his kingdom, how many people lived in each district, and how rich or poor they were.

Officials were sent to each parish. They questioned the reeve (the man who looked after the lord's land), the parish priest and six peasants in each manor, writing down what they were told. A second group of officials then checked the written descriptions to prevent errors or corruption. The whole task was finished within a year, an amazing achievement considering the poor state of communications.

Most of William's subjects were not impressed. They hated what was being done – rightly suspecting that it would lead to higher taxes. What business did a king have counting their possessions? But the survey could not be avoided, like death, and that is how it came to be called the **Domesday Book**.

The information collected by William's officials suggests a total population of 1.5 to 2 million. About 9 per cent of those recorded were slaves and held no property; 32 per cent were called 'bordars' or 'cottars' and held only 5 per cent of the total area of land: 55 per cent were named as 'villeins' or freemen, owning 65 per cent of the land. This left the most wealthy 3 per cent, the king, his barons and the Church, holding 30 per cent of the land – and the best land too.

The Conquest had not destroyed the prosperity of England. More than 13,000 settlements were recorded in the Domesday survey. Almost all of these were rural, the homes of people who earned their living from the land. More than 6,000 flour mills, and various small industries like lead mining in Derbyshire and salt production in Worcestershire, were also recorded.

Extracts from the Domesday Book are given in Sources A – C.

Source A

Shipley in Yorkshire

'In Shipley, Ravenchil held one hide in the reign of King Edward. There was room for two ploughs and it was worth ten shillings. Now it is waste. Robert de Lacey owns it.'

*A **hide** was an amount of land.*

Population in 1086 shown in the Domesday Book.

Number of people per square mile

- ■ over 10
- ▨ 2.5 – 10
- □ under 2.5
- ----- Limit of Domesday survey

Source B

Birmingham (then a tiny village)

'Richard holds Birmingham from William. There is land for 6 ploughs; there is one plough in the demesne. There are 5 villeins and 4 bordars and 2 ploughs. There is a wood half a mile long and 4 furlongs broad. In the time of King Edward it was worth 20 shillings, and it is still worth the same.'

Villeins and *bordars* were types of peasants. *The demesne was the lord's land; 4 furlongs is about 800 metres.*

Source C

Brooke in Norfolk

'Brooke was held by Earl Gyrth in the time of King Edward, and King William gave it to the abbey of St Edmund. There were then 33 villeins; now 38. Then as now 3 slaves. Now 3 ploughs on the demesne and 6 ploughs belonging to the men. Woodland for 30 pigs; 9 acres of meadow. Now 5 horses, 14 beasts, 40 pigs, 65 sheep and 20 goats.'

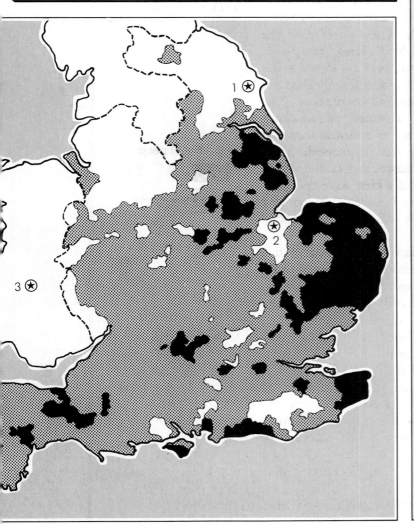

Questions

Section A

1 The officials who carried out the survey must have had a common set of questions which they had to ask in each parish. Using Sources A–C, try to work out what the questions were.

2 We have seen from the Domesday Book how much land was held in 1086 by the slaves, the bordars or cottars, the villeins or freemen, and by the king, the barons and the Church.

   a Using the percentages given, display this information in the clearest way you can. You might use a table, a pie chart, a bar chart, cartoons or any other method.

   b What does your diagram tell you about Norman England?

3 Trace the map showing population density in 1086.

   a How does the distribution of population in 1086 compare with today?

   b Explain why the areas marked ★ had very few people according to this map.

Section B

4 Write a list of all the things which historians could use the Domesday Book as evidence for.

5 Historians need to know whether their sources are accurate and complete. Do you think that the Domesday Book was an accurate survey? Give reasons for your answer.

6 Do you think that the following statements about the Norman Conquest are true? Give evidence from Sources A–C to support your answers.

   a There had been many changes in land ownership since the Norman Conquest.

   b The Conquest had not destroyed the prosperity of England.

Who Killed William Rufus?

William I was the ruler of a state that stretched both sides of the English Channel. At his death his state was split in two. The Conqueror's eldest son, Robert, inherited Normandy; and his second eldest, William, inherited England. Many of the barons who had lands on both sides of the Channel were not happy at finding that they now had to serve two different rulers.

In 1088 a group of these barons rebelled against William II. They hoped that Robert would be able to land an army from Normandy and reunite the two parts of the Conqueror's kingdom. This revolt failed, as did another in 1095. But for as long as England and Normandy had different rulers it was likely that some barons would support a rebellion to unite the two countries.

William II, who was called William **Rufus** because of his red face, came close to reuniting the two parts of his father's kingdom. After the failure of the rebellion of 1095, Robert decided he would join the Crusade that was being organised. (The Crusades were a series of wars in which the European Christians tried to recapture Jerusalem from the Turks.)

Robert needed a lot of money if he was to join the Crusade, and he borrowed it from William Rufus. They agreed that while Robert was away Rufus was to rule both England and Normandy. If Robert returned, and repaid the loan, then Rufus would give Normandy back to him. The two men also agreed that if one of them should die, the other would inherit both parts of the kingdom.

During the next five years William Rufus was a successful king. He quarrelled with some of the leaders of the Church, but otherwise seems to have been well accepted on both sides of the Channel. He was capable of being cruel, and the descriptions of his character, such as Source A, suggest that he was an unpopular man.

William Rufus died in 1100. He was shot while hunting in the New Forest (Hampshire). The man who fired the arrow was probably Walter Tirel, who was one of William's companions on the hunt. The circumstances of his death are mysterious, and various theories have been put forward.

Theory A: It was an act of God. William was being punished for his poor treatment of the Church.

Theory B: It was an accident. Tirel, aiming at a deer, missed.

Theory C: It was an assassination plot. Henry (William's younger brother) arranged for William to be murdered so that he could become king.

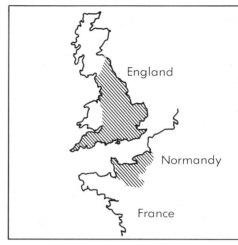

England and Normandy in 1100.

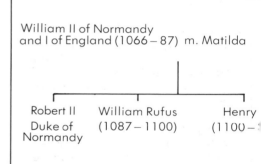

The family tree of William Rufus.

Source A

'He was very harsh and fierce in his rule, and towards his followers and all his neighbours, very terrifying. Influenced by the advice of evil councillors, who were always agreeable to him, and by his own greed, he was continually upsetting this nation with unjust taxes. He oppressed the Church of God; and in his days when a bishop or an abbot died, he either sold the lands for money, or kept them within his grasp and let them for rent. Everything that was hateful to God and to good men was the daily practice in this land during his reign. Therefore he was hated by almost all his people and abhorrent to God.'

From a chronicle written by a monk soon after William Rufus's death.

Activity

Each of the statements below could be used as evidence to support one of the theories. For each statement, work out which theory you think it supports and why.

1 William had a dream the night before he died which suggested he would be killed.

2 Henry was with the hunting party.

3 Hunting accidents were common in Norman times. Two important nobles had been killed in hunting accidents during William's reign.

4 Tirel fled the country and never returned.

5 St Anselm, the Archbishop of Canterbury, who was in France because of his quarrel with William Rufus, claimed he knew immediately the king died because an angel told him.

6 Henry moved very quickly after William's death. The same day he rode to Winchester and claimed the royal treasure. Within three days he rode to London, persuaded the most powerful nobles that he should be the next king, and was crowned.

7 No writer at the time suggested that William's death was murder.

8 More or less Henry's last chance to take over both parts of the kingdom was in 1100. Robert was on his way back from the Crusade, and when he got back he would be the next king if William Rufus died.

Questions

Section A

1 The beginnings and endings of the following sentences have been mixed up. Match the correct heads and tails.

Heads	Tails
Two of William I's sons, Robert and William Rufus,	he borrowed money from William and went on a Crusade.
Many barons were not happy about this	William was killed, and Henry ruled both England and Normandy.
Robert, William I's eldest son,	each inherited part of his kingdom.
William Rufus	because they had land in both England and Normandy.
Robert failed to invade England so instead	was given England.
Just before Robert came back from his Crusade	had the lands in Normandy.

Section B

2 Do you think the monk in Source A is a trustworthy witness about William Rufus?

3 Which of the theories about William Rufus's death seems best to you? Explain the theory, backing it up as well as you can.

4 Which of the theories about William Rufus's death seems the worst to you? Explain why.

5 'There can be no doubt that William Rufus was murdered and that Henry was behind it.' Do you think this statement is true or false? Give reasons for your answer.

Motte and Bailey Castles

Dinan's Castle, showing the motte, from the Bayeux Tapestry.

The first castles that the Normans built and lived in were not the large, stone-built castles which still survive. Usually, the Normans built their castles out of materials that were easy to get, cheap and quick to use. Stone was none of these things – but wood and earth were. So most early castles were made from wood and earth. They are called **motte and bailey castles**.

The **motte** was a big mound of earth, a man-made hill. The **bailey** was a large flat area defended by ditches and walls. The bailey was used for keeping animals and storing food, and much of the day-to-day business of the castle was done there.

There are no motte and bailey castles left today. Some just rotted away, others were destroyed in war, most were replaced by more up-to-date castles. This means that the big problem for the historian is to find out what they were like. All sorts of sources can be used:

archaeology – the sites of some castles have been dug up;
landscape – the castles have left some remains;
pictures – the Bayeux Tapestry shows two motte and bailey castles;
documents – some people wrote descriptions of these castles.

By using all these different sources we can start to work out what motte and bailey castles were like.

Weaknesses of motte and bailey castles

Source A gives a clue about the most important weakness of a motte and bailey castle if it was attacked. It was made of wood, so it could be set on fire. There were other problems as well. There was usually only a small space at the top of the motte. You can see just how small the space was by looking at the scale in Source D. Living in such a small area must have been cramped and uncomfortable. Also wood, if put in earth, will rot in time. So after fifty or more years motte and bailey castles would need a lot of rebuilding.

Because of the weaknesses of motte and bailey castles the Normans gradually replaced them with stone-built castles, which overcame most of these problems.

Activities

1 The following statements are either true or false. Copy them out and explain which you think they are, using Sources A and C as evidence.

   a The motte had a wall built round the top.
   b The motte had a tower or house on top of it.
   c The motte was surrounded by a moat.
   d The motte was so steep you needed a bridge to get up to it.

2 Find and explain four ways in which Source B agrees with what Sources A and C show us about mottes.

3 Does Source B tell us anything that we did not find out from Sources A and C?

4 Draw Source D. Using what you have learnt about mottes from Sources A, B and C, see if you can join up the dots to make a plan of the top of the motte. Label your drawing.

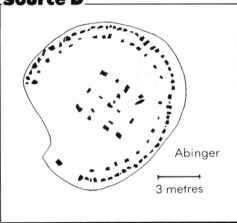

Source B

'It was the custom to heap up a mound of earth as high as they were able, and to surround the whole upper edge of the mound with a barrier of wooden planks, stoutly fixed together with numerous turrets set round. Within was built a house, or rather a citadel. The gate of entry could only be reached by a bridge.'

From a description of the motte at Mershem in France, written by Jean de Colmien in the eleventh century.

Source C

The Castle of Rednes (now call Rennes), showing the motte, from the Bayeux Tapestry.

Source D

Abinger

3 metres

This drawing shows what the archaeologist found on top of the motte. Each of the black dots is where a wooden post had been driven into the ground.

Questions

Section A

1 Draw a diagram of, and describe, a motte and bailey castle.

2 What were the problems of motte and bailey castles?

3 Which of the problems was the most important? Give reasons for your answer.

Section B

4 What could you learn from Sources A, C and D which the written source did not tell you?

5 What could you learn from the written description (Source B) which the other sources did not tell you?

6 What could you learn from the archaeological plan (Source D) which the other sources did not tell you?

7 Why do historians try to compare different types of sources?

The Site of a Castle

When a Norman baron arrived in the lands he had been given by William after the Conquest, the first thing that he would usually do was to build a simple castle. This was because there were usually very few Normans in the area, but a great many Saxons. Although Harold had been killed and the Saxon army was defeated, there was hatred of the new lords which would take many years to go away. In his armour, on his horse and surrounded by his soldiers the baron had nothing to fear; but he could not spend all his life on horseback. The barons needed somewhere they could be very safe – safe even from their own peasants.

It was important to build this castle in the right place. The exercises in this unit look at the decision which the first barons had to take. Where, in their area, should they build their castle?

Problem one: in which part of his lands should the baron build the castle?

There are a number of different factors which the baron had to think about before making his choice:

1 **Availability of materials.** The castle needed to be built as quickly and cheaply as possible. As it was a motte and bailey castle, the materials needed were earth and wood.
2 **Availability of labour.** Motte and bailey castles needed lots of labour, especially to dig the earth and make the mound.
3 **Access to main routes.** The baron needed to keep in contact with the king and the rest of the county.
4 **Ease of reaching all villages in the area.** The baron needed to keep in close contact with all his lands, to collect rents and to enforce the law.
5 **Place of refuge.** If the area should be attacked, the baron's castle was the place where as many people as possible would come for protection. The easier it was to reach, the better a refuge it would be.

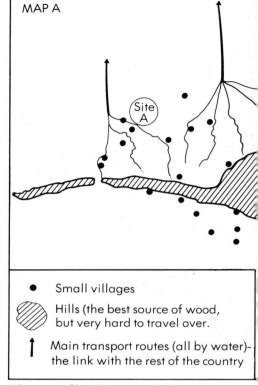

MAP A

● Small villages

▨ Hills (the best source of wood, but very hard to travel over.

↑ Main transport routes (all by water)- the link with the rest of the country

The area of land given to the baron.

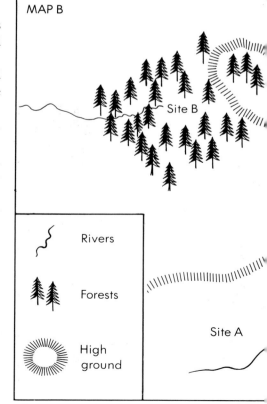

MAP B

Site B

〰 Rivers

🌲 Forests

☀ High ground

Site A

The possible sites.

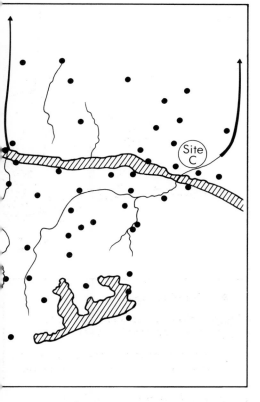

To decide where the baron should build his castle, copy the following table into your book and fill it in. Consider each factor for all of the sites shown on Map A, and give each site a mark out of ten. If the site is a good one for that factor, give it a high mark. When you have finished, total the marks for each site.

	Site A	Site B	Site C
Availability of materials:			
Availability of labour:			
Access to main routes:			
Ease of reaching all villages:			
Place of refuge:			
Total:			

Problem two: *the exact site of the castle*

Having decided in which part of his lands to build a castle, the baron then had to decide on the exact site. On a hill or in the town or village? In different parts of the country the Normans made different choices. In Canterbury some houses were pulled down, and the castle was built in the city; in Dover the castle was built on the hill overlooking the city.

This time the factors the baron had to consider were different:

1 **Ease of access.** As it was the baron's home, he needed a castle that was fairly easy to get to.
2 **Access to water.** Water was needed for day-to-day life in the castle. If the castle was ever besieged, it would be vital to have a good water supply.
3 **Command of the routeways.** The baron needed access to the other parts of his lands and the rest of the country. If the castle site gave a view down some of these routeways for some miles, so much the better.
4 **Natural strong-point.** Some places are easier to defend than others. A good view of the surrounding area, so that an enemy could not approach the castle unseen, and a site not easily overlooked, were the most important things.

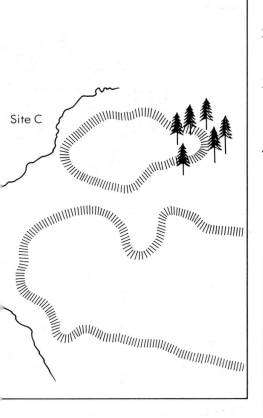

Question

Copy out the following table and fill it in, giving each site on Map B a score for each factor.

	Site A	Site B	Site C
Ease of access:			
Access to water:			
Command of routeways:			
Natural strong-point:			
Total:			

The Square-keep Castle

Castle Hedingham in Essex. How did the builders of the castle solve the problem of defending the windows?

Some square-keep castles had been built in England from the time that the Normans first settled. Square keeps cost much more money and took more time to build, so at first there were very few. To start with only the most important towns, such as London, had square keeps. But when the Normans decided that it was time to replace the wooden motte and bailey castles, square keeps became much more common.

The two great problems with motte and bailey castles had been that they were cramped, and that they could be too easily attacked by fire. Making the castle out of stone meant that much larger castles could be built, and at least the outside of the castles would be fireproof. Stone is much heavier than wood. In fact, stone is so much heavier that a square keep could not possibly be built on a motte – it would be too heavy, and both the motte and the keep would collapse. This meant that a square keep had to be built on the ground. However, being at ground level, it was easier to attack. The builders of square keeps had to find ways of making them harder to get into, because that is what attackers would be trying to do.

The secret of the square keep was its walls. The main ways of attacking a castle were to use battering rams, or even picks, to make a hole in the wall. To stop this the walls of a square keep were as thick and strong as possible, sometimes as thick as 7 metres.

Castles, though, were not just used for fighting; they had to be lived in during peacetime. Unless there were some windows, the castles would be miserable places to live in. And unless there was a door, it would not be possible to live in them at all! Both doors and windows would be holes in the walls; and as the main defence of the castles was that the walls kept people out, windows and doors were obviously a problem.

The most important primary sources for historians of castles are the castles themselves. Many square-keep castles have survived; some in ruins, and others much changed from when they were first built. By careful study of what remains it is often possible to work out what the castle was originally like. Later walls can be spotted because different stones were used to build them, or because they were built in a different way. From the castles, plans and photographs, it is possible to get a good idea of how the problem of windows and a door were solved.

Questions

Section A

1 In what ways were square-keep castles an improvement on motte and bailey castles?

2 As square-keep castles were safer than motte and bailey castles, why did the Normans not build only square-keep castles?

3 Why were square-keep castles built with such thick walls?

4 What were the defensive problems of square-keep castles? How were they overcome?

Source B

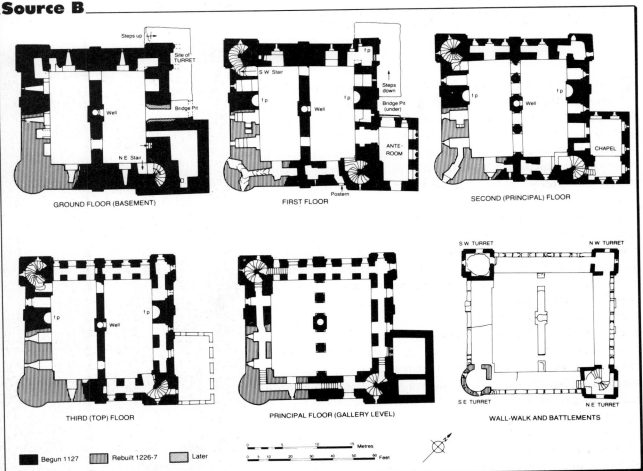

Plans of Rochester Castle. The thick black sections are the original walls. The sections shaded in with lines are walls that were rebuilt later, and the section marked with dots is a modern hole in the wall.

Section B

5 Could you prove that the following statements are true by using the evidence of buildings?

a People in the Middle Ages were just as interested in war and killing as people in the twentieth century.

b There were military secrets in the Middle Ages just like there are today.

c Every person in the village would be proud of the local castle that kept them safe.

Activities

1 Describe the route that someone would have to take to get inside the castle. The only door was through the anteroom on the first floor.

2 What chances would the defenders have to attack the people trying to get in through the door?

3 How is the castle protected against people climbing in through the windows?

4 Compare Sources A and B. Have both these castles solved the problem in the same way?

The Feudal System

Just building castles did not solve the problems of the Normans in England. King William and his followers were unwelcome foreigners who had conquered the country and started to make their homes there. Building castles meant that these homes were as safe as the Normans could make them; but a castle would be no use without soldiers to guard it. Also, William would need an army of soldiers in case there was a major rebellion or if an enemy force invaded.

The most important type of soldier was the **mounted knight**. William would not be safe unless he could call on a large number of mounted knights. One way of getting knights was to have them live as part of his household. The problem was William would then be responsible for feeding them and providing all the equipment and horses the knights would use. This would be far too expensive. Not even the king could afford to pay for knights sitting around all the time when he didn't need an army, just to make sure that he would have an army when he did need one. The **feudal system** was the way that William and the later Norman kings solved this problem.

Because William had become king by conquering England, he was able to claim that the whole country belonged to him. All the land, no matter who had owned it before the battle of Hastings, was part of his prize for winning. William kept a great deal of land himself. The rest of the land was divided up among his followers. However, he did not just *give* these men their land. William, in theory, still owned all the land, and people who were given land became his tenants. Like modern tenants, these people had to give something in return for their land – a type of rent.

Each of William's most important followers became a **tenant-in-chief** (sometimes called a **baron**). This meant the man got his land directly from the king. In return for land each baron owed the king military service. The baron would have to provide a number of knights to guard royal castles for a set number of days each year. The baron would also have to provide knights for forty days if William wished to raise an army and go to war. The tenants-in-chief could raise the number of knights they owed the king either by having them live in their household and paying for them; or by having sub-tenants. A sub-tenant was a knight who in return for part of the baron's land would agree to be one of that baron's knights for a set number of days in the year. As well as being used by the baron to 'pay' his debts to the king, the knight would also be used to guard the baron's castle and be part of his escort on important journeys.

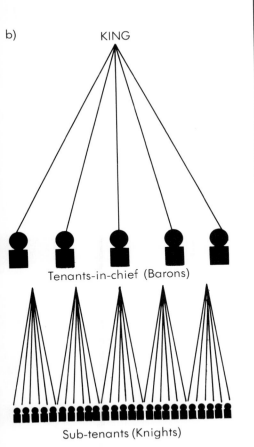

a)

KING

give soldiers to · gives land to

BARONS · BARONS

give soldiers to · give land to

KNIGHTS

b)

KING

Tenants-in-chief (Barons)

Sub-tenants (Knights)

In all there were about 1400 tenants-in-chief and about 8000 sub-tenants.

The feudal system.

Questions

Section A

1 Why did Norman kings need to have plenty of soldiers available?

2 Why could the king not just keep the soldiers he needed as part of his household?

3 Copy the following paragraph and fill in the blanks from the list of words provided below:

The feudal system was similar to the modern idea of ..... houses. The king gave large estates to his ..... . These people did not pay any money for their lands, but instead their 'rent' was to provide the king with a number of knights who could serve in his ..... . The tenants-in-chief were able to provide ..... because they had the same type of arrangement with the knights. The knights got ..... from the tenants-in-chief in return for giving a set number of days' service.

money	knights	tenants-in-chief
army	bishops	kitchens
land	renting	court

4 Explain the advantages that you think each of the following would have got from the feudal system:

a the king;
b a tenant-in-chief;
c a knight.

Section B

5 Each of the following sentences might be a *cause* of the introduction of the feudal system. Copy each sentence into your book and explain why you think it was, or was not, a cause.

- The Normans had just conquered England.
- Many knights were not very nice people to spend your days with.
- The horses and equipment of a mounted knight were very expensive.
- William wanted to reward the people who had helped him conquer England.
- Harold and most of the Saxon leaders had been killed at Hastings.
- William wanted to make sure the Norman baron would stay loyal to him.
- The feudal system was practised in Normandy, so William and his barons were used to it.
- England was a rich country.

The Church

There were two important parts to the Church both before and after the Norman Conquest. There were parish priests who lived in the villages and towns, and who were responsible for services in the local church. There were also monks and nuns who lived in special communities apart from the rest of the people. This separation was to allow the monks and nuns to live as close as possible to the ideal way that Christians should live.

All the services of the Church were in Latin, the ancient language of Rome. The parish priests needed to be able to speak Latin, and also to read it well enough to be able to hold services. However, the local priest was not always well educated. There were many cases of priests who could not read at all, and who were just giving church services from memory. Before the Conquest the Church in England had not been as strict as the Pope felt it should have been. Most of the parish priests were married, although they were not supposed to marry.

If not all priests could read as well as they were supposed to, hardly anyone who went to their church could read at all. Not only were most people unable to read, they were also unable to understand in any detail what was going on in the service because it was in Latin. This meant that pictures were very important in getting people to understand about the Christian faith. Source A is part of a wall-painting from a Norman church.

The life of the parish priest, who was often poor and worked on the land in much the same way as his parishoners, was very different from that of the monks and nuns. The

Source B

Alkborough Maze, Humberside. Mazes like this were used by Christians of the Norman period to symbolise the soul's journey through earthly life to heaven.

Source C

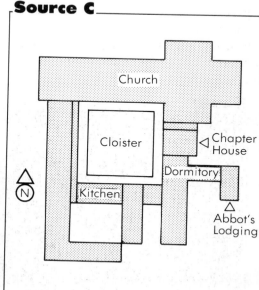

Plan of Byland Abbey, North Yorkshire.

Source A

Part of the painting called the Great Doom, at Chaldon, Surrey. It shows some of the horrors of hell: a miser is being roasted, cheating traders are suspended over the fire on a bridge of spikes.

monks and nuns lived in their own communities, where everything was organised around worship. After the Conquest the English monasteries followed a timetable for the day and rules for behaviour that were first set down by St Benedict in the sixth century. A typical monk's day:

Time	Activity
02.00	Get up, first church service of the day.
04.00	Church service.
05.00	Private reading and prayer.
06.00	Church service followed by breakfast.
07.00	Work.
08.00	Church service.
09.00	Chapter (a meeting), followed by work in the cloister.
11.45	Church service followed by a meal.
13.00	Private reading and prayer.
14.45	Church service.
15.00	Work.
17.45	Meal, followed by church service.
19.15	Private reading and prayer.
19.45	Church service.
20.00	Bed.

Most of the old abbeys in which the monks and nuns lived were rebuilt by the Normans, and many new ones were founded. The Normans also rebuilt many cathedrals and parish churches. In their size, design and decoration these churches were grander than the Saxon buildings they replaced. From large, purpose-built abbeys to small parish churches the Normans created buildings which have been admired ever since.

Source D

St Albans Abbey.

Questions

Section A

1 What were the main differences between the parish priests and the monks and nuns?

2 Why were wall-paintings very important in Norman churches?

3 Copy the Alkborough Maze (Source B). Solve it in your book.

4 Why do you think monks and nuns lived in special religious communities?

5 Draw a time-line for a monk's day.

6 Draw a plan of Byland Abbey (Source C). Show by adding labels which parts were used at which times during the day.

Section B

7 How do you think a parish priest would feel about the way monks spent their days?

8 What effect do you think the Great Doom at Chaldon (Source A) would have on the peasants who saw it?

9 Do you think there is a connection between the ideas behind the Great Doom and the Maze? If so, what is it?

10 Sources C and D are buildings. Can they tell us anything about the way the Normans felt about God? Explain your answer.

The Village and Open-field Farming

The most important thing in most peasants' lives was the **manor**. The manor was the area of land owned by the local landlord. This usually included a village and some farming land, as well as the lord's own house or castle. The manor was the land given to a sub-tenant under the feudal system. The man granted the manor was called the '**lord of the manor**' and had special rights in law over all other people who lived there. Each manor had its own court, where the rules were enforced, and a steward who organised the farming of the lord's land, and kept the records about who owed what for their land.

The peasants who lived on the manor could not leave it without the lord's permission. They had to work on the lord's lands in return for their own plots of land and houses. The peasants lived in a village which had the farming land around it. There were usually three large fields for growing crops. Each field was divided up into small strips which belonged to different people. The richer peasants had several strips and the poorer peasants only one or two. The lord of the manor had the largest number of strips; his strips often included the better land.

If the same crops are grown on the same land year after year, the crops get poorer and poorer. The crops grown in the three fields were changed each year to avoid this. One field was used for wheat, one for barley and one left fallow (with nothing growing on it). Changing the crop in each field every year, and having the field lie fallow once every three years, stopped the soil from becoming exhausted. This also meant everyone had to grow the same crops in the same field. As well as their strips in the three fields, all villagers were allowed to keep animals on the common land, and also to collect fuel there. This was very important, especially for the poorest villagers who did not have enough land in the strip system to keep them fed.

Farming was very hard physical work at this time. There was no source of power other than muscle power, supplied either by horses and oxen or by the people themselves. The ploughs did not break up the soil to any great depth. Seeds were sown by the 'broadcast' method – that is, thrown by hand from a bag carried round the neck. When it was time to harvest the corn, gangs of peasants, each with their scythe, were needed. This was a slow and hard job. There was also the added fear that, if the weather spoilt the crop before the harvest was safely collected, the community would face food shortages, or even starvation, during the winter.

Norman farmers from the Bayeux Tapestry

A carving from Barfreston Church, Kent, showing a manor steward.

An aerial photograph of Lower Ditchford, Gloucestershire, a medieval village which was later deserted. You can still see the site of the streets, and the ridges and furrows that divided the field into strips.

The harvest.

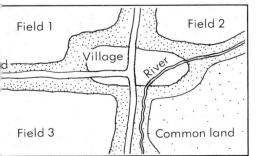

...-field farming.

Questions

Section A

1 Match up the following heads and tails:

Heads	Tails
Manors were units of land	divided into three fields and common land.
Peasants were given land	and peasants had strips in each field.
There was a manor steward	into which the countryside was divided.
The farming land was	in return for working on the lord's land.
Each field was divided into strips	with only simple tools and animal power.
Work on the land was hard	who kept the records about what each person owed.

2 Make three copies of the open-field farming diagram and show which crops would be grown in each field each year.

3 Draw each of the farming tools you can see in the sources. Write a sentence suggesting what each one was used for.

Section B

4 Study Source A. Work out which part was the village and where the fields were (look for changes in direction of the furrows). Trace the outline of the village and where you think the fields were.

5 Divide your page into two columns. Where you can find some evidence in the sources which supports the text, copy the part of the text which is supported in the left-hand column and the source that supports it in the right-hand column. For example:

The peasants would live in a village with farming land around it.

Source A – this shows where the village was and the fields around it.

6 Copy the following statements. In each case explain whether you think it is true or false on the evidence of the sources.

   a All Norman ploughs had two wheels and were pulled by one animal.
   b Different peasants would use scythes with different-length handles.
   c Harvesting was done in gangs of six.

97

Henry Tudor and the Battle of Bosworth

Henry Tudor led the last successful invasion in English history. His invasion, which happened in 1485, was not like the invasions of the Romans, Saxons or Normans. Each of these invasions had been by a group of foreign people who settled in, and changed, England. Henry Tudor, however, was a British nobleman – but one who had lived in exile for some years. His success in 1485 did not bring the enormous changes that the previous invasions had caused.

Henry Tudor landed in Wales with a small force, which he hoped to increase by recruiting in England. When he got to Bosworth he had between 5,000 and 6,000 men. Henry hoped to meet up with the forces of the Stanley family; but, although they were in the area, they would not join him. Richard III was holding one of the sons of the family hostage and neither he nor Henry Tudor could be sure which side the Stanleys would fight on in the battle. The Stanleys had about 5,000 men. Richard III had raised troops as soon as he heard that Henry had landed, and had between 10,000 and 12,000 men with him at Bosworth.

The battle of Bosworth game – rules

The game is to be played by three players: Richard III, Henry Tudor and Stanley. The game is over when either Richard's army or Henry's army is defeated. The game aims to reproduce the uncertainty of the outcome of the battle.

Richard III: Richard's army has three pieces. Cavalry, commanded by Richard, strength 2 points. Infantry, commanded by Norfolk, strength 6 points. Infantry, commanded by Northumberland, strength 3 points.

Henry Tudor: Henry's army has two pieces. Cavalry, commanded by Henry, strength 1 point. Infantry, commanded by Oxford, strength 5 points.

Stanley: The Stanley family's forces have two pieces. Infantry, commanded by Lord Thomas Stanley, strength 3 points. Cavalry, commanded by Sir William Stanley, strength 2 points.

Turns: The game starts with Henry Tudor's turn, then Richard's, then the Stanleys'. Each player can move all, some or none of their pieces. A player can either move or fire infantry pieces.

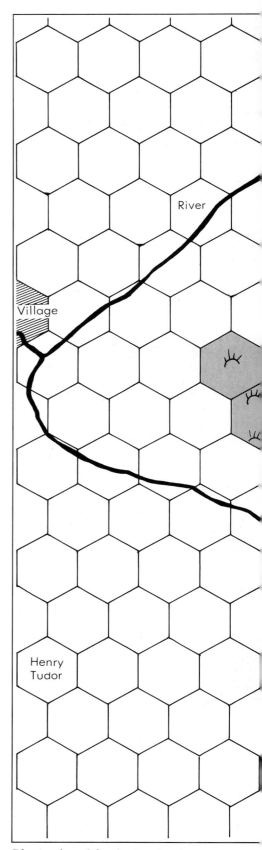

Playing board for the Battle of Bosworth gam...

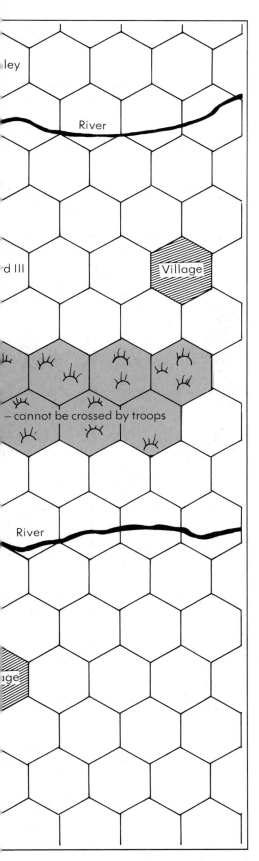

Strength: Make a table in your book showing the strength of each of your pieces. Keep this table up to date by taking points away when your piece is shot at or loses a fight.

Movement: Cavalry can move two spaces per turn. Infantry can move one space per turn.

Firing: The range of an infantry piece is one space. If enemy pieces are within a space they can be fired on, and the enemy piece's strength is reduced by one.

Fighting: If two pieces, not on the same side, are in the same square, they are fighting. The players should toss a coin, then compare the strengths of the two pieces and add two points to the side that won the toss. The side with the highest number of points wins. The losing side takes one point away from the strength of the piece involved.

What really happened

Henry did not know what the Stanleys would do, but attacked anyway. His infantry attacked Norfolk's section of Richard's army, but were slowly being beaten. Henry's only chance was if the Stanleys joined in on his side. He rode off with his cavalry to appeal to them. Richard saw this as his chance and charged Henry's cavalry with his own, leading the charge himself and killing Henry's standard-bearer. At this point the Stanleys attacked Richard's cavalry, and he was killed. Not only did the Stanleys desert Richard, but also Northumberland, who commanded the third section of his army, did nothing to help him and took no part in the battle.

Questions

Section A

1 Describe each of the armies that met at Bosworth.

2 Draw three plans of the battlefield and show the development of the battle on them. Label the armies and add notes to help explain what was happening.

3 Why do you think Henry Tudor won the battle of Bosworth?

Section B

4 Compare the result of your game with other games in your class.

    a Did they get the same result?
    b Why do you think this was?

5 Do you think it was inevitable that Henry Tudor would win the battle?

6 Has the game helped you understand what happened? Explain your answer.

Henry VIII

Between the battle of Bosworth in 1485 and his death in 1509 Henry VII did as much as he could to make sure that the Tudors would keep the throne. Prince Arthur, Henry VII's elder son, died in 1501; but there was another son, also called Henry, who could succeed to his father's throne. Henry VII did much to re-establish law and order in England after the problems of the Wars of the Roses, and was very successful at improving the royal finances. When he died his son Henry inherited the kingdom and a royal treasury that had plenty of money in it.

Henry VIII became king in 1509 when he was seventeen. He was king for 38 years. When he died in 1547 not only had he had six wives, but he had also changed the religion of his country, fought successful wars and emptied the royal treasury. Henry has been one of the most talked about monarchs ever since. Some have said of him:

'All Europe admired his talents as scholar, poet, musician and sportsman. In spite of the fate that awaited them women were eager to marry him and men to serve him. He was a true prince of the Renaissance.'

Others have had a very different view:

'*Question:* Was he a good king? *Answer:* No, he was one of the worst kings that ever reigned in England.'

One of the quotations above is from a modern textbook, and one from a nineteenth-century textbook. Can you work out which is which?

Sources A–F show some of the different sides of Henry's character, and the different reactions he provoked in people.

Source A

'The king (who is most wise and watchful in everything) is in the habit of handing over books which he does not want to read himself to one of his courtiers to go through. From him he afterwards learns their contents. He then takes them back and gives them to be examined by someone else of an entirely opposite way of thinking. And when he has thus found out from them, and what they like and dislike, he at length openly says what he thinks.'

Written by Thomas Cranmer, later made Archbishop of Canterbury by Henry.

Source B

'His Majesty said, "Talk with me awhile. The King of France, is he as tall as I am?" I told him there was but little difference. He continued, "Is he as broad?" I said he was not. He then inquired, "What sort of leg has he?" I replied, "Spare." Whereupon he opened his doublet, placed his hand on his thigh and said, "Look here; I also have a good calf to my leg."'

Written by the Venetian Ambassador to England, 1518.

Source C

Two suits of armour, both made to fit Henry VIII.

Source D

A picture of Henry VIII painted during the early part of his reign.

Source E

Questions

Section A

1 What advantages did Henry VIII have when he became king?

2 There are four achievements of Henry VIII mentioned in the second paragraph. Which do you think he would regard as successes and which do you think he would regard as failures? Give reasons for your answer.

Section B

3 Which of the following words best sums up Henry's character according to Source A: vain/sensible/short-tempered/stupid? Explain your answer.

4 Which of the following words best sums up Henry's character according to Source B: vain/sensible/short-tempered/stupid? Explain your answer.

5 How can you explain the difference between the suits of armour in Source C?

6 Which of the figures in Source F is Henry? Give reasons for your answer.

7 Which of the three paintings of Henry (Sources D, E and F) do you think Henry VIII would choose as the best? Explain your answer.

8 Which of the paintings (Sources D, E and F) would you choose as the best to illustrate a book about Henry VIII? Give reasons for your choice.

9 How can you explain so much disagreement between sources about one person?

10 Which sources do you think might be unreliable and why might they be unreliable?

A picture of Henry VIII painted near the end of his reign.

Henry VIII jousting.

Source F

Cardinal Wolsey

Thomas Wolsey did not start life as the son of a powerful noble family. His father was a butcher in Ipswich. Wolsey was a very clever young man, who got his university degree at the age of fifteen, and soon attracted wealthy patrons. This was the usual route to success for the able sons of poor families. A **patron** was a nobleman with great wealth and power, who would use these to help men whom he found useful. Wolsey's first patron was the Marquis of Dorset. When he died (in 1501), Wolsey moved to the service of Sir John Nanfleet, a powerful officer in the king's service. Wolsey became Nanfleet's personal chaplain in 1503, and in 1507 became chaplain to King Henry VII.

This was a very quick rise to an important position. After Henry VII died in 1509, Wolsey continued to serve his son, Henry VIII. Soon after the new king came to the throne Wolsey was made a member of his Council – the people who actually governed the country. Unlike his father, Henry VIII did not want to spend all his time governing the country, and Wolsey quickly gained Henry's trust as a person who would do a lot of the work for him. In 1513 Henry declared war on France, and Wolsey was largely responsible for raising the army and planning the campaign. The war resulted in victories against the French, and against their allies, the Scots. Wolsey got most of the credit for this, and in 1514 Henry made him Bishop of Lincoln, Bishop of Tournai and Archbishop of York all in the same year. As Wolsey held all these jobs at the same time, this meant he did not have enough time to do each one of them properly. Most of his time was still spent working for the king. The advantage of so many jobs was that each had a large salary. Wolsey was a very rich man.

Wolsey continued to be Henry VIII's most important minister. He virtually governed England in the king's name, and Henry continued to reward him on a lavish scale. In 1515 he was made a cardinal, in 1518 Bishop of Bath and Wells, and Papal Legate (the Pope's personal representative and therefore head of the Church in England). In 1521 Wolsey became Abbot of St Albans (England's richest monastery), and two years later Bishop of Durham. Finally, in 1528 he was made Bishop of Winchester.

Wolsey fell from power in 1529 because he failed to arrange Henry VIII's divorce from Catherine of Aragon. He died in 1530 while travelling to London under arrest for treason. During his years in power he had made many

Source A

'This Wolsey with his pride and ambition aroused the hatred of the whole country against himself. He was hostile to the nobles and to the common people. He was loathed by everyone because he thought he could carry out all the offices of state by himself. Wolsey carried out all business just as he liked, because the king valued him more than anyone else.'

★ ★ ★ ★

'Wolsey, acquiring so many offices at almost the same time, became so proud he considered himself the equal of kings. He soon began to use a golden chair, a golden cushion on his table, and to have the hat, symbol of the rank of Cardinal, carried before him.'

★ ★ ★ ★

'He was also not satisfied with the one cross which he had used in his capacity as Archbishop of York, but would have another carried before him by two priests riding on great horses who were bareheaded at all times of the year. This vanity, vainer than any ever known before, provoked both amusement and irritation in all.'

Three extracts from 'Anglica Historica', a history of England written by Polydore Vergil, an Italian historian who lived in England for many years during the reigns of Henry VII and Henry VIII.

enemies. People said he was arrogant, and many nobles found it hard to forget he was a butcher's son. The following sources give different views about what this very successful man was like.

Questions

Section A

1 Draw up a time-line showing the main events in Wolsey's life.

2 Describe Wolsey's rise to power.

3 Why was it lucky for Wolsey that Henry VII died and was replaced by Henry VIII?

4 A pluralist was someone with more than one position in the Church.

 a Was Wolsey a pluralist?
 b Why might people object to pluralism?
 c Was pluralism the only thing about Wolsey which would upset people?

Section B

5 Which of the three authors of the sources disliked Wolsey the most? Give a reason for your answer.

6 Compare Sources A and D. How does Source D back up Source A?

7 Polydore Vergil (Source A) was imprisoned on Wolsey's orders. George Cavendish (Source B) was one of Wolsey's servants. Does this information help you to decide whether the sources are reliable?

8 Do you think Source C is more or less likely to be reliable than Sources A and B?

9 What sort of person do you think Wolsey was? Give reasons for your answer.

Source B

'In honour, triumph and glory, Wolsey reigned a long season. By his wisdom he ruled all things in this realm through the king. He also dealt with all weighty matters of foreign relations.'

From a life of Wolsey written by George Cavendish.

Source C

'The Cardinal is very much admired and respected. He has a very fine palace, where one has to go through eight rooms to reach the audience room.'

A description of Wolsey written by the Venetian Ambassador in a secret report sent to Venice.

Source D

Wolsey setting out on a journey.

The Reformation and the Dissolution of the Monasteries

At the start of the sixteenth century there was only one Christian Church in Western Europe – the Roman Catholic Church. This state of affairs did not continue for long. In 1517 a German priest, **Martin Luther**, published criticisms of the Catholic Church which were so serious that he started a breakaway Church not under the Pope's control. These events did not have a large impact on England at first, but relations between the Pope and Henry VIII deteriorated during the late 1520s and early 1530s.

In 1533 and 1534 Henry made England a Protestant country through a series of Acts of Parliament. In 1536 this 'Reformation' was taken a stage further when the smaller monasteries were dissolved (closed down). The dissolution of the remaining monasteries and the publication of a Bible written in English followed in 1539.

The Reformation was possibly the most important change in England and Europe during the sixteenth century. Some people were so horrified by it that they revolted against Henry's rule; others were executed rather than accept Henry's changes. Historians have been keen to explain the causes of such an important event, but they have not always agreed with one another about what those causes were. We are going to look at four different factors which may have been causes of the English Reformation.

Theology

The **theology** of a religion is the collection of its most important beliefs. Martin Luther was not the first person to criticise the ideas of the Roman Catholic Church, but his criticisms found many supporters. His most important criticism was that the Catholic Church had developed away from the the way the Church was set up in the Bible. He also criticised the power of the Pope, and the luxurious lives led by some Churchmen. Luther believed that the Bible should be the basis of all Christian faith and that as many people as possible should be able to read the Bible in their own language.

Source A

A popular cartoon. Two devils blow evil ideas into the Pope's head while others deal with the monks.

Divorce

It was very important to every king at that time that he had a healthy son to succeed to the throne when he died. To have no children, or to have only daughters, meant there was a great risk of civil war breaking out after the king's death. Most people believed then that only a man could control the powerful nobles.

In 1527 Henry VIII had two problems. Catherine of Aragon, his wife since 1509, was too old to have any more children, and only one of their children, a girl called Mary, had lived. The second problem was that Anne Boleyn, whom Henry was attracted to, had refused to become his mistress and insisted that he would have to marry her. He decided that for the sake of the country he would divorce Queen Catherine and marry again so that he could have sons.

Under the Roman Catholic Church only the Pope could grant a divorce. Between 1527 and 1529 Henry tried to get the Pope to agree to a divorce for him, but he refused. Henry continued to look for ways to change the Pope's mind until, in 1533, he had the Archbishop of Canterbury grant him a divorce.

Money

Henry VIII had been involved in a number of wars in Europe, all of which had been expensive. Henry could not raise enough money by taxes and was always looking for extra sources of money. In 1535 he ordered an investigation into the wealth of the monasteries which was called the *Valor Ecclesiasticus*. This showed that the monasteries owned about one quarter of the land in England.

Unpopularity of the Church

The Catholic Church was unpopular with many people. It was felt that the Church was too often interested in money rather than faith. Monks and nuns came in for special criticism, because many people felt that rather than living pure and simple lives, as they should, they lived luxurious and corrupt ones. The investigation of the monasteries in 1535 produced many reports like this one: 'The Prior a very virtuous man, but his monks more corrupt than any others in vices. Some monks have ten women, some eight.'

Questions

Section A

1 Draw a time-line showing the years 1510 to 1540. Mark on it the important events in the story of the Reformation.

2 What were the main theological criticisms of the Catholic Church?

3 Why did Henry VIII feel he needed a son?

4 Why was Henry's divorce a religious problem?

5 Why did Henry need money?

6 How did Henry know about the wealth of the Church?

7 Why was the Catholic Church unpopular?

8 Do you think the Catholic Church was unpopular with everyone?

9 Study Source A. What are the monks standing in? Why was this part of the joke?

Section B

10 Historians sometimes divide causes of events into long-term and short-term causes. Short-term causes explain why the event happened exactly when it did. Are any of the four causes in the text (theology, divorce, money and the unpopularity of the Church) short-term causes?

11 Is there any connection between the four possible causes listed above?

12 Do you think one of the possible causes was more important than the others? If so, which? Give reasons for your answer.

The Castles of Henry VIII

Throughout his reign Henry VIII involved England in wars with France and the Holy Roman Empire – at the time the two strongest countries in Europe. After the Reformation, England was a Protestant country, but France and the Empire were Roman Catholic. The Pope tried to interest these two countries in an invasion of England to restore Catholicism. When the Pope first suggested the idea, France and the Empire were at war with one another, so they were not interested in an attack on England. In 1538, however, the two countries signed a ten-year truce.

There had been only one or two castles built in England during the previous hundred years. Why did Henry build so many in such a short space of time? This section shows how well we can answer that question by using the evidence of the castles and the weapons that were to be used in them.

While they are not all the same, Henry's castles were all similar to one another. They were all built of stone and low in height; they got the most firepower by building the middle sections taller, so defenders could fire over the outer walls.

Source A

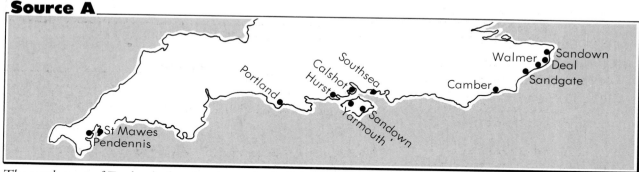

The south coast of England, showing the castles built by Henry VIII.

Source B

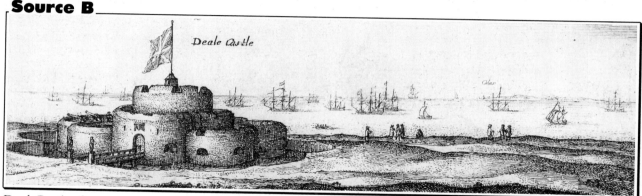

Deal Castle, from a seventeenth-century print.

Source C

A cross-section through Deal Castle, showing the gun positions.

One of the main differences between these castles and the Norman castles we have already looked at is that Henry VIII's castles were built after gunpowder was used in the West. The castles were built to survive attacks by cannon, and to use both cannon and hand-held guns for defence.

Activities

1 What was Henry VIII worried about after 1538?

2 Look at Source A. What common feature do all Henry's castles share?

3 Does the connection between Henry's worry and the common features of the castles help you to decide what job they were intended to do?

4 Look at Sources B and C. Can you decide how Henry thought his castles would be able to do the job?

5 Some of the defences of the castles were to protect them against attack from enemy troops if they should land. List the defences Deal had against attack by soldiers on land.

6 The diagram (below) of the arc of fire of each gun shows how you can work out how the castles were protected. Copy either of the plans from Source D and mark on the arc of fire for each gun position.

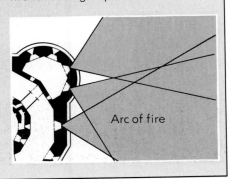

Arc of fire

Source D

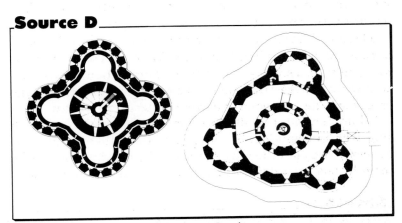

Plans of Hurst Castle and Walmer Castle.

Questions

Section A

1 Give two reasons why Henry VIII felt the need to protect England.

2 Why were the castles of Henry VIII different from earlier castles?

3 Copy the cross-section of Deal Castle. Give each gun a label. Say whether it is a musket or a cannon, and suggest what its main target might have been.

Section B

4 Copy each of the following statements and then, using the evidence you have, say whether you think they are true or false:
  a The castles of Henry VIII were very carefully designed.
  b part of the plan to defend Deal Castle would be to flood the moat if there was a danger of an attack.
  c The castles would be easy targets for attacking cannon.
  d The castles were built inland because Henry feared a Roman Catholic rebellion.

Religion in the Reign of Edward VI

When Henry VIII died, his son, Edward, became king. However, Edward was only nine. A young child could not rule the country himself. Most of the work usually done by the king was done by one of Edward's uncles, the Duke of Somerset. Somerset was a convinced Protestant who thought that the changes made in the Church after the Reformation had not gone far enough. With the support of the young king he set about making England a more Protestant country.

In the sixteenth century everybody who lived in England was a Christian. There were no people of other faiths, such as Hindus or Muslims, and no people who did not believe in God at all. As well as believing in heaven, people in the sixteenth century also believed in hell. They felt those people who did not live proper Christian lives would go to hell, which was a place of everlasting torture and torment.

Sixteenth-century Christians believed that the *way* they worshipped God was important, and that if they worshipped God in the wrong way they would be likely to go to hell rather than heaven. Until the Reformation all people in England had worshipped in the same way, the way of the Roman Catholic Church. After the Reformation the Church services were changed a little, but they were still very similar to the old services.

The Roman Catholics believed that the Pope should be head of the Church, and that religion should be based on both what the Pope said and what the Bible said. They held their church services in Latin, with the priest dressed in splendid and costly robes. The churches were decorated with paintings and stained-glass windows, with the altar in the east, and with statues of saints and of the Virgin Mary.

Protestants believed that religion should just be based on the Bible. They wanted nothing to do with the Pope. They wanted church services in English, with the priest dressed in plain and simple robes. They also thought that churches should be as plain and simple as possible, without any painting or statues at all.

After Henry VIII made England a Protestant country he made the churches hold their services in English, but did not change anything else.

How do you think people who preferred the Catholic type of services would have felt about Henry VIII's version of Protestantism?

How do you think a convinced Protestant would have felt about Henry VIII's version of Protestantism?

A sixteenth-century view of hell.

The Duke of Somerset and Edward VI made the following changes to the English Church to make it more Protestant:

1547   Statues and pictures ordered to be removed from churches.

1547   Book of Protestant sermons printed which had to be read in all churches.

1549   Prayer Book with new services for all churches introduced. The changes included moving the altar to the centre of the church, plain clothes for the priest and an end to parts of the service that were just English translations of the old Catholic services.

Activities

Look carefully at Source B and then answer the questions.

1 Who is the figure in the bed?

2 Who are the people at the bottom on the left, and what is happening to them?

3 What is happening out of the window?

A painting with a political message. Edward VI is seated on the throne, with his Council seated at the table. The Pope is wearing the pointed hat.

Questions

Section A

1 Copy out the following paragraph. Where you come to the words in brackets, choose one of the alternatives.

In the sixteenth century all (Christians/Catholics) believed in hell. They believed if they did not worship God (every Sunday/in the right way) they would go to hell when they died. This meant that the way that church services were held mattered to (both Catholics and Protestants/just Protestants) very much.

2 Make a list of the differences between Catholics and Protestants during the reign of Edward VI.

Section B

3 How do you think people who preferred the Catholic-style services would have felt in 1547 after they heard of the changes in the Church?

4 How do you think people who preferred the Catholic-style services would have felt when they first went to a service held by the rules of the 1549 Prayer Book?

5 In 1549 there was a rebellion in Devon and Cornwall against Edward VI. Here is an extract from the demands of the rebels:

'We wyll have the holy decrees of our forefathers kept and performed. ... We will have the masse in Latten, as was before. ... Images to be set up again in every church.'

a What do you think people who preferred the Catholic-style services would have thought about the demands of the rebels?

b What do you think Protestants would have felt about the demands of the rebels?

6 Do you think that Source B was painted for a Protestant or a Catholic? Give reasons for your answer.

The Reign of Mary I

Queen Mary was the eldest daughter of Henry VIII. After her brother Edward VI died in 1553, she became queen before Elizabeth, Henry's other daughter. Mary was at first welcomed by her new subjects. Straight away she changed the way the English Church was run, making it much more like the old Roman Catholic Church. Next, in 1554 she planned to marry King Philip of Spain. Spain was one of the most powerful countries in Europe, and one of the most Catholic. There was a revolt against Mary and this marriage, but it was easily defeated.

In November 1554 Mary and her new husband made England part of the Roman Catholic Church again. The next year Mary began the part of her reign that is always remembered, **the persecution of the Protestants**. People who would not rejoin the Roman Catholic Church and accept the Pope as its head were imprisoned, sometimes tortured; and if they still refused, they were burnt at the stake. Between 1555 and 1558, when Mary died, about 280 people were burnt, including a number of the bishops who had been the leaders of the Church during Edward VI's reign.

Source A

ACTES
and Monument
of these latter and perillous dayꝭ
touching matters of the Church, where
ar comprehended and described the great perſe-
tions & horrible troubles, that haue bene wrou
and practiſed by the Romiſhe Prelates, ſpecia-
lye in this Realme of England and Scot-
lande, from the yeare of our Lorde a
thouſande, vnto the tyme
nowe preſent.

Gathered and collected according to th
true copies & wrytinges certificatorie, as we
of the parties them ſelues that ſuffered, as
alſo out of the Biſhops Regiſters,
which wer the doers therof,
by Iohn Foxe.

¶Imprinted at London by Iohn Day,
dwellyng ouer Alderſgate.
Cum priuilegio Regię Maieſtatis.

Part of the title page from the 1563 edition of Foxe's 'Book of Martyrs'.

Source B

The burning of Latimer and Ridley, two of Edward VI's bishops. The picture is taken from Foxe's book.

Source C

Bishop Bonner, one of Mary's Catholic bishops, whipping a Protestant in the garden of the bishop's palace. The picture is taken from Foxe's book.

The story of the people who were burnt during Mary's reign was told in a very famous book written at the time by a Protestant who escaped abroad. The book has a very long title (as you can see from Source A); it is usually called Foxe's *Book of Martyrs*. This was the second most popular book in England for the next hundred years (the most popular was the Bible). A large number of people in Tudor England could not read; but books were read out loud, and the pictures could be seen by all.

Questions

Section A

1 Draw a time-line showing the events in Mary's reign mentioned in this unit.

2 Mary changed the religion in England in two stages.

  a What was the first change?
  b What was the second change?
  c Why do you think she split the changes up like this?

3 Mary's persecution of people who did not agree with her religious ideas was not unusual in the sixteenth century. Yet Mary has a reputation as a fanatic. Can you suggest any reasons for this?

Section B

4 One of the problems historians face with older documents is simply being able to read them. Copy out the words from the title page of Foxe's book (Source A).

5 Do the words on the title page make you think that Foxe might be biased in any way? Quote the words you think prove that Fox was biased or unbiased, and explain *why* they prove it.

6 Does Source B give any clue about whether the crowd agreed with the burning, or whether they were against it?

7 Are the following statements true or false? In each case copy out the statement, say whether it is true or false, and then give reasons for your answer.

  a Sources A, B and C prove that Protestants were cruelly treated during Mary's reign.
  b Sources A, B and C prove that Foxe hated the Roman Catholics?
  c Sources A, B and C do not prove anything. Sources B and C are pictures and they could have been made up.

Queen Elizabeth I

One of the problems historians have to deal with is **hindsight**. Hindsight is knowing how events in the past turned out in the end, which people at the time could not know. *We* know that Elizabeth I was one of the most successful rulers that England has ever had, but people did not know that when she became queen in 1558.

England in 1558 was not an easy country to rule. There had been rebellions against Henry VIII, Edward VI and Queen Mary. In the previous twenty-five years the country's religion had been changed several times. To add to the problems, Elizabeth was a woman, and most people in the sixteenth century felt that women were inferior to men. This meant that they did not like taking orders from a woman, or obeying laws that had originally come from a woman. The problems of Queen Mary's reign had probably made more people unhappy about the idea of a woman ruler.

Two years after Elizabeth became queen, one of the members of her government remembered what England had been like when she came to the throne:

'I never saw England weaker in strength, men, money and riches. As much as I love my country and my countrymen, I assure you I was then ashamed of them both. They went to the wars hanging down their heads. They came back men dismayed and forlorn. Here was nothing but fining, heading, hanging, quartering and burning. A few priests ruled all.'

Elizabeth managed to overcome all the problems she inherited. While she was queen (from 1588 to 1603) England survived attacks from foreign countries, and developed into a strong and secure nation. Elizabeth found an answer to the religious problems. She set up a Church which was a compromise between the very Protestant Church of Edward's reign and the Roman Catholic Church of Mary's reign. Her Church was the beginning of the present-day Church of England. We do not remember Elizabeth's reign just for her political successes, though. This was also the age of Shakespeare and Drake, Spencer and Raleigh.

What did Queen Elizabeth look like?

Historians often try to answer very difficult questions such as why a war started, or why major changes in society happened. Let us see what happens if we ask a simple question: What did Elizabeth look like? After all, everyone who ever met Elizabeth would be able to answer the question.

Source A

Elizabeth, painted in 1560.

Source C

Elizabeth, painted around 1600.

Source B

Elizabeth, painted in 1588 to celebrate the defeat of the Spanish Armada.

Source D

'Queen Elizabeth's hair was more reddish than yellow. She asked me what colour of hair was thought best; and whether my queen's hair or hers was best; and which of them was the fairest. She asked which of them was the tallest. I said my queen. Then, said she, she is too high; for I am myself neither too high nor too low.'

A description of a conversation in 1564 between Elizabeth and the Ambassador from the Queen of Scotland.

While Elizabeth was queen she had her portrait painted many times. There were no newspapers or television. Travel took a long time and was fairly rare. Many people could see the queen only through paintings, which she was careful to make sure were sent all round the country. This means we have plenty of evidence from which to work out what Elizabeth looked like.

Questions

Section A

1 Copy out the following sentences, matching the heads and tails.

Heads	Tails
We know that Elizabeth I was a great queen because	and Elizabeth's sister Mary had made things worse during her reign.
This is called	in 1558 people would have been very worried.
When Elizabeth came to the throne	hindsight.
The country had many problems	we know what happened in her reign.

2 Why was religion a problem for Elizabeth?

3 Why was being a woman a problem for Elizabeth?

4 Can you explain why there are so many paintings of Elizabeth?

Section B

5 Which source gives the clearest picture of Elizabeth?

6 Do you think paintings or written descriptions will be the more useful source to someone trying to work out what Elizabeth looked like?

7 Elizabeth was born in 1533 and died in 1603. How old was she when each of the sources is describing her?

8 Do you think the paintings are reliable sources of evidence about Elizabeth's appearance?

9 Why do you think the paintings make Elizabeth look the way she does?

10 Is finding out what Elizabeth looked like simple or difficult? Explain your answer.

Entertainment I: Primary Sources

During Elizabeth's reign **theatres** were built in London, and plays were performed in them that have interested people ever since. These were the first theatres built in Britain since Roman times. It would not have been worth building theatres unless there were a lot of people who wanted to watch plays, and unless those people also had the time and money to do so. The cheapest way of watching a play was to stand on the ground around the stage. This cost one penny. People who wanted seats went into the galleries round the outside of the courtyard. This cost more, but there were advantages: it was more comfortable, you would not get wet if it started to rain and, most important for some, people would look at you, so you could show off your fine clothes. The plays that were put on had to interest all sorts of people. Many wanted a simple story with plenty of action, others wanted poetry and fine speeches, so most plays had both.

Source A

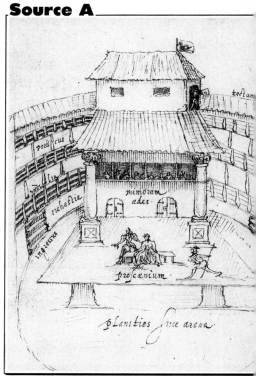

The inside of the Swan Theatre, drawn by a Dutch visitor to England in 1596.

Activity

Look through the texts of some Elizabethan plays and count up the number of killings and fights on stage. Good plays to try are Shakespeare's *Julius Caesar*, and *Titus Andronicus*, or Christopher Marlowe's *Tamburlaine* and *The Massacre at Paris* (which was for some time the most popular play in Elizabethan London).

The outside of the Globe Theatre and another building used for bear-baiting ('beere bayting'). This print was published in 1647 from drawings made a few years earlier. In the printing a mistake was made; the building labelled the Globe was in fact the one used for bear-baiting, and the one labelled bear-baiting was the Globe.

Source B

Source C

From the papers of Philip Henslowe, who put on both plays and animal-baiting shows.

Source D

'The framework of the theatre to be made square and to be 80 foot square [about 7.5 m²] outside and 55 foot square [about 5 m²] inside. And the framework to be three floors in height, all of which shall contain four rooms for gentlemen's rooms, and other divisions for two-penny rooms, with the necessary seats to be placed and set in these rooms, and throughout all the rest of the galleries, as are made in the Globe playhouse recently built.

With a stage and tiring house, with a cover over the said stage. The stage shall be in length 43 feet [about 13 m] and in width extend to the middle of the yard of the house.'

From the contract to build the Fortune Theatre, 1600.

Plays were not the only public entertainment in London. There were various types of animal fights and these also drew large crowds. The same buildings were often used for both animal fights (called baiting) and for plays. You can see how similar the two buildings in Source B are. Source C is a poster which was used to advertise one day's animal-baiting.

While Queen Elizabeth and many people liked the plays, there were others who did not. Some very religious people known as Puritans thought that the plays, and the actors themselves, were bad and sinful. Others worried that the large crowds would cause trouble, and that thieves would concentrate around theatres. Pickpockets were believed to work among the audience. Even worse than this was the danger of spreading plague – which in a bad year killed many people in London. The City Council thought that plague was spread to different parts of the city when people collected together to watch plays. In bad plague years the theatres were closed for weeks at a time.

Questions

Section A

1 Where had plays been performed before theatres were built?

2 Study Sources A and B. Imagine you were a traveller visiting London for the first time. Write a letter describing English theatres to someone who had never seen them.

3 What were the different places in the theatre from which people could watch the play? Give an advantage and a disadvantage of each place.

4 Use Source D to draw a plan of the Fortune Theatre which is to scale. Label the different parts of the building.

5 Why did some Elizabethans object to the theatre?

Section B

6 Copy out Source C.

7 Does the poster make you want to see the show? Give reasons for your answer.

8 Do you think the poster would make Elizabethans want to see the show? Give reasons for your answer.

9 Do you think Elizabethans must have been cruel people to watch such shows? Explain your answer.

Entertainment II: Secondary Sources

N o Elizabethan theatre has survived. Historians have had to work out what they were like from pictures such as Sources A and B; from descriptions of the theatres by one or two travellers who visited them; and from a few other documents. The most useful of these is the contract to build the Fortune Theatre (Source D).

In this unit we are going to look at the problems of deciding what Elizabethan theatres were really like. We need to remember that there were a number of theatres in Elizabethan London, and they might not all have looked the same. The evidence in the last unit, comes from three different theatres: the Globe, the Fortune and the Swan. We need to look for common features shared by these theatres.

Note

This unit uses sources A, B and D from The Tudors 5.9 on pages 114–15.

Activities

1 What is the difference between Sources A, B and D, and Sources E, F, G and H?

2 Make a list of the sources in this unit according to how realistic you think they are.

Before looking at the sources in this unit in more detail, look again at the primary sources on pages 114–15. Once you see how much the primary sources tell us, you will be in a better position to judge how realistic the secondary sources are.

Activity

Copy out the following table and complete it by studying Sources A, B and D.

	Source A	Source B	Source D
Size:			
Galleries:			
Stage:			
Tiring house (building behind the stage with dressing rooms, etc.):			
Stairs to galleries:			
Seats:			

Source E

The Globe Theatre from the outside.

Source F

The inside of the Globe Theatre.

Source G

Another reconstruction of the inside of the Globe Theatre.

Sometimes the sources do not tell us as much as we would like. For example, none of them tells us about the entrance from the street. However, using common sense, we know that there must have been one. There is no reason to believe that Sources A, B and D are not reliable, but even so a historian has to work quite hard to interpret the sources to make a reconstruction. You can see how different the reconstructions made in Sources E–H are. What you are going to do next is to judge which is the best by comparing each of them with Sources A, B and D.

Source H

The Fortune Theatre.

Activities

1 Draw up a table like the one below. This time you are going to list the things that are in the reconstructions, but for which you can't find evidence in Sources A, B and D.

Source	Things for which there is no evidence in Sources A, B and D	Conclusion: was this something that should have been put in?
F	1 Flag on top of the roof.	Yes. Source D shows one on the bear-baiting; it might have been advertising.

2 Look at the list you made earlier in which you put Sources E–H in their order of realism. Would you change the order at all?

Questions

1 Which of Sources E–H do you think is the best version of what an Elizabethan theatre might have looked like? Give reasons for your answer.

2 Can you be sure that everything about the one you have chosen is completely correct? Explain your answer.

3 Do you think the following statement is true or false? Give reasons for your answer. 'Historians have an easy job. They just have to find the right sources and then they can solve all their problems.'

So far you have used the primary sources to work out as much as you can about Elizabethan theatres. The primary sources have also helped you to judge which of the secondary sources is the best reconstruction. This does not mean that when primary sources and secondary sources disagree, the primary are always right. In this case, we have primary sources which are not biased; but sometimes a primary source may have to be ignored because it cannot be trusted.

Sir Francis Drake's Voyage around the World

While Elizabeth was queen, English sailors made many daring voyages to different parts of the world. They were usually trying to increase the country's trade; either by finding new places to sell English goods, or by finding new places to buy goods needed in England, or both. Sometimes the sailors attacked other Europeans they met on their voyages, particularly the Spanish. Spain claimed it was the only country allowed to trade with America, and Spain was also the chief Roman Catholic country in Europe.

One of the most famous Elizabethan sailors is Sir Francis Drake. His voyages show the mixture of trading, fighting and great skill in seamanship which was typical of Elizabethan sailors. In question 3 you are asked to look at one of Drake's voyages in detail.

Drake's voyage round the world.

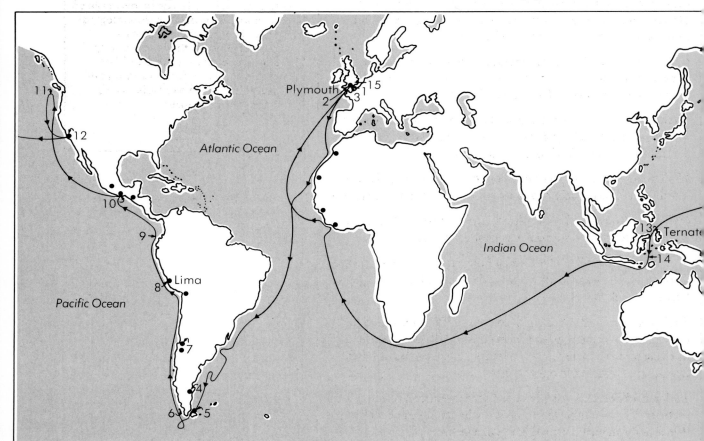

Drake's voyage, 1577–80

November 1577: five ships were ready to leave Plymouth – the *Pelican*, *Benedict*, *Marigold*, *Swan* and *Elizabeth*.

5 December 157?: Valparaiso was the first Spanish American town Drake raided. Wines and some gold and silver captured.

17 June – 23 July 1579: Drake found a bay to anchor his ship in and rested and reprovisioned the *Golden Hind* before trying to get home by sailing across the Pacific.

15 November 157?: A bad storm just after they started sent all five ships back to England for repairs.

20 August 1578: Before entering the Straits of Magellan, Drake renamed his ship the *Golden Hind*, hoping a new name would change his luck.

13 December 1577: The repairs were finished and the fleet sailed again.

11 May 1579: The weather was too cold to sail any further north. Drake gave up the idea that there might be a way home round North America and sailed back the way he had come.

June – August 157?: There was nearly a mutiny before the fleet got to Cape Horn. Drake thought his friend Thomas Doughty was causing the trouble; he had him executed. Two of the ships, the *Benedict* and the *Swan*, were abandoned after their crews and stores had been transferred to the other three.

8 January 1580: The *Golden Hind* ran aground. Some spices and some of the cannon were thrown overboard to make the ship lighter. This worked, and the *Golden Hind* sailed on.

(*Number 6 on map*) Bad storms as they came out of the Straits of Magellan sank the *Marigold* and separated the *Golden Hind* and the *Elizabeth*. The *Elizabeth* sailed back to England.

15 February 157?: When he captured the Port of Lima, Drake heard that a treasure ship had sailed for Panama ten days before.

(*Number 10 on map*) 13 – 14 April 1579: Drake landed all his Spanish prisoners and started to look for a way home.

3 – 9 November 157?: The *Golden Hind* reached an island called Ternate where Drake made a treaty with the local chief and got ten tons of valuable spices.

26 September 1580: Drake arrived back in England. His first question was whether Queen Elizabeth was still alive. If she had died a new monarch might have been trying to make friends with Spain, and Drake could have been in trouble.

1 March 157?: Drake caught up with the treasure ship. He pretended his own ship was a Spanish ship and sailed very close, then shot down the treasure ship's main mast.

Questions

Section A

1 What were Elizabethan sailors usually trying to do on their voyages?

2 Why did Elizabethan sailors sometimes get into fights with the Spaniards?

Section B

3 Copy the map of Drake's voyage into your book. The route that Drake's ship took has been marked, and there are arrows pointing to places where major events happened. From the list of events given in the box (which have been mixed up, and which sometimes do not have a complete date), work out what happened at each stage of Drake's journey. Then write up the events in the correct place on your map. Drake's voyage lasted from 1577 to 1580. Two of the events have been given their numbers as clues.

4 The map exercise was an example of putting events in their **chronological** order. How useful are dates to historians when they are working out chronological problems? Use your own experience in sorting out question 3 as an example to help explain your answer.

The Spanish Armada

Which of these policies will you choose?

a Send more troops and ships to your American colonies. *(GOTO A1)*
b Send more troops to the Netherlands. *(GOTO B2)*
c Invade England. *(GOTO C3)*

M ost people know something about the story of the Spanish Armada, the fleet that Philip II of Spain sent to invade England in 1588. Like all events in history the sailing and defeat of the Armada involved a lot of separate choices made by various people. Choices were made by Philip and his advisers, by Elizabeth and her advisers, by admirals and captains, and even by individual sailors. The first part of this unit takes you through an exercise where you have to repeat some of these choices.

What shall we do next...?

Work in pairs or in fours. Some choices are to be made by the English and some by the Spanish. Try not to look at the results of your choice until you have made it. In real life people can never be sure exactly what the result of their actions will be.

Decision one: Spain

You are Philip II of Spain. You have called a meeting of your advisers because you are worried by the English. There are four problems:

1 English sailors (like Drake) are raiding your ships and towns in America and you are losing a lot of treasure.

2 There has been a revolt in the Netherlands, part of your empire. The people in the revolt want to be independent from Spain. They also want to be Protestants rather than Catholics. Queen Elizabeth is giving them money to buy arms to fight your troops.

3 You are a very religious man and a Roman Catholic. You would like all countries to be Catholic and you would like to stop England being a Protestant country.

4 If Elizabeth was no longer Queen of England, and was replaced by a Catholic, no one knows who that person should be. Until last year it would have been Mary Queen of Scots, but Elizabeth has had her executed.

Decision Two: England

You hear that Philip II is getting a fleet together to attack England. What will you do?

a Wait and see what happens. *(GOTO A4)*
b Stop all attacks on Spain's American colonies. Imprison all your great sailors like Drake. Stop helping the revolt in the Netherlands. Hope all this will be enough to call off the attack. *(GOTO B3)*
c Attack the Spanish fleet before it leaves Spain. Try to delay it so you can improve your defences. *(GOTO C1)*

Decision three: Spain

King Philip now needs a plan. He must land enough troops in England to beat the English army. Most of his troops are in the Netherlands with the Duke of Parma.

Philp has two plans he can choose from. Which would you choose?

a Send his fleet (the Armada) along the English Channel until it can pick up Parma's army from Calais. Then use the Armada to take the army across the Channel. *(GOTO A2)*
b Send Parma's army across the Channel on whatever small boats Parma can find. Do not worry about the English fleet. *(GOTO B1)*

Decision four: England

The Armada has been seen coming towards the Channel.

Which of these plans should the Council of War follow?

a Follow the Armada, attacking any ships which fall behind, and trying to stop it landing. *(GOTO A3)*
b Risk everything in an all-out battle. *(GOTO B4)*
c Pick the place where the Armada is most likely to land and defend it. *(GOTO C4)*

Decision five: Spain

You are now the Duke of Medina Sidonia, commander of the Armada. Your fleet has got as far as Calais. The Duke of Parma sends a message that he will be at least another week.

What do you do?

a Wait. (GOTO A5)
b Try to invade England with the very few troops you have on board. (GOTO B6)

Decision six: England

You are running out of supplies. The Armada is safe at harbour in Calais. You call a Council of War at sea.

Which of the following policies will you try?

a Fill some small ships with things that will burn and set light to these ships (fireships). Let the tide take the fireships into the Spanish fleet. (GOTO C2)
b Wait until night, then send fireships to wreck the Armada. (GOTO B5)
c Wait until the Armada sails from Calais and then attack it. (GOTO C5)

Questions

Section A

1 Describe the story of the Armada as it came out in your game. Who won? What were the important decisions and why did you make them?

2 Your teacher will tell you the choices that were made. Describe what really happened using the information in the decision sections to help you.

Section B

3 Are the following true or false? Explain your answer.

a The Spanish lost only because they made bad choices.
b It does not matter what people wanted or what people chose to do in history.
c It was inevitable that the Spanish Armada would be defeated. (This means no other result was possible.)

Results

A1 The attacks carry on and there are even bigger problems in the Netherlands. Go back to decision one.

A2 This might work. Go on to decision four.

A3 You cannot stop the Armada, but you do capture a couple of ships. Go on to decision five.

A4 Go to decision three.

A5 There is not much else you can do. Go on to decision six.

B1 This is a disaster. The English fleet sinks most of Parma's ships while they are at sea and cannot defend themselves. Your attempt to invade England fails, and you lose the Netherlands because you have lost most of your army.

B2 You manage to keep things fairly quiet in the Netherlands, but cannot afford to keep this many soldiers there any longer because your losses from English raids in the Americas go up. Go back to decision one.

B3 Spain does not call off the attack. You cannot defend England properly, as most leaders of the navy are in prison. The Spanish land troops and conquer England.

B4 The Armada outnumbers your fleet. You are defeated, and there is nothing to stop the Armada landing Parma's army. England is invaded.

B5 This is what the English did and it was very successful. The Armada began its long journey right round the British Isles to return to Spain. Storms sank many more ships than the English did. The country is safe from invasion.

B6 You do not have enough troops. Your invasion is defeated on the beaches of Kent.

C1 Good idea. Drake's raid slowed the Spanish down by a year. Go on to decision three.

C2 This is almost what the English tried. The difference is that they waited until night. Historians have suggested that the added confusion of darkness really caused the Spanish to panic. The Armada survives your attack with the loss of a few ships. It is strong enough to take Parma's army over the Channel when Parma is ready. England is invaded.

C3 This will not be easy but it is probably the best you can do. Go on to decision two.

C4 Look at the map of the south coast. Pick the area you will defend and then go on to decision five.

C5 The English fleet had failed to stop the Armada sailing the whole length of the Channel. It would have failed to stop it crossing the Channel at this narrow point. England is invaded by Spanish troops.

Poverty in Elizabethan England

It is easy to make the past seem much better than it was. It is easy to concentrate on the good and successful things and to miss out the bad things. There were many problems in Queen Elizabeth's reign as well as many successes. One of the problems that people at the time were worried about was the increasing number of poor people.

At the start of Elizabeth's reign there was nothing like our modern Welfare State. People who could not work and who did not have any money had to rely on charity. Often they had to beg. It would not be much use being a shy beggar, hidden away from the crowds, so poor people begging were very noticeable in Elizabethan towns. This may be one of the reasons why the Elizabethans were so worried by the problem of poverty.

Elizabethans divided poor people into two sorts. People who were poor through no fault of their own were called the **impotent poor**. This would include those who were ill or unable to work because of injury, and widows looking after their children. People who were fit to work but did not have a job were called **sturdy beggars**. The impotent poor were treated fairly well, but this was not always the case with sturdy beggars. Most Elizabethans believed that they did not have jobs because they were lazy rather than because there were not enough jobs. While the impotent poor were given charity, the sturdy beggars were treated harshly. The punishments changed during Elizabeth's reign but included whipping, burning through the ear and even hanging.

One of the few things sturdy beggars could do to find a job was to move from one part of the country to another. This caused even more problems. They were then classed as **vagrants**, people with no home or job. Vagrants usually went to towns, because that was the best place to find a job. The towns, though, tried to get rid of vagrants. If they stayed in the town and didn't get a job, the people in the town would have to pay to keep them alive. Worse still, most people thought that vagrants were not only lazy, but also criminals. Laws were passed against vagrants. These laws listed various types of vagrants: as well as beggars there were soldiers and sailors returning home, pedlars, tinkers, actors, jugglers, palm readers, keepers of dancing bears, minstrels, students and wizards.

It was not until Elizabeth's reign was nearly over that the way people thought about poor changed. People came to realise that there were some who just couldn't find work. A

turn to page 124

Drawings of beggars in the sixteenth century.

Source B

'Beggars, not wanting to get their living by the sweat of their brows, will wander in their wicked way through most of the counties of England. Although they are punished by stocks, whippings, and imprisonment they like their lewd lecherous loiterings so much these are soon forgotten. An unruly rascal may go to a man's house and demand charity, either claiming he had served in the wars and was maimed or that he is looking for work. If he is offered meat and drink he will refuse it and take only money, and if he sees young pigs or poultry he notes the place and the next night, or shortly after, he will be sure to steal them.'

From a popular book, written by an Elizabethan magistrate in 1567.

system was set up to raise money for the poor. The impotent poor no longer had to beg, and the sturdy beggars would be found work and, if necessary, somewhere to live.

Source C

'This day was brought into the court one Mother Arden who used daily to go begging in the streets. She was found to have:

in old groats	£29.13s.4d [£29.67]
two old angels [coins worth nearly £1 each] in counterfeit money	£9.16s.6d [£9.83]
in new money	£3.13s.7d [£3.68]'

From the records of Norwich, giving details of cases tried by the mayor of Norwich.

Questions

Section A

1 Why do you think Elizabethans were worried about the number of poor people?

2 What was the difference between the impotent poor and the sturdy beggars?

3 How would the impotent poor have been treated?

4 How would the sturdy beggars have been treated?

5 How would books like Source B affect people's attitude to beggars?

Section B

6 Imagine you are the Mayor of Norwich, and you have read books like Source A.

   a How would you treat a healthy man who said he had walked from London to Norwich to look for a job?
   b How would you treat Mother Arden?
   c How would you treat the people in Source A?

7 We do not nowadays punish people who cannot get a job by whipping them or burning their ears. Does this mean Elizabethans were deliberately cruel?

You
nosie
Bastard

Kiss
me
please ♡